Nick Vandome

iPad
for Seniors

In easy steps is an imprint of In Easy Steps Limited
4 Chapel Court · 42 Holly Walk · Leamington Spa
Warwickshire · United Kingdom · CV32 4YS
www.ineasysteps.com

Second Edition

Notice of Liability
Every effort has been made to ensure that this book contains accurate
and current information. However, In Easy Steps Limited and the
author shall not be liable for any loss or damage suffered by readers
as a result of any information contained herein.

Trademarks
iPad® is a registered trademark of Apple Computer, Inc. All other
trademarks are acknowledged as belonging to their respective
companies.

In Easy Steps Limited supports The Forest Stewardship Council (FSC),
the leading international forest certification organisation. All our titles
that are printed on Greenpeace approved FSC certified paper carry the
FSC logo.

FSC
www.fsc.org

MIX
Paper from
responsible sources

FSC® C020837

Printed and bound in the United Kingdom

ISBN 978-1-84078-583-8

Contents

1 Choosing your iPad

It's small, it's stylish, it's powerful, and it's perfect for anyone, of any age. This chapter introduces the iPad and covers the basics so you can quickly get up and running with this exciting tablet computer.

The iEverything

The iPad is a tablet computer that has gone a long way to change how we think of computers and how we interact with them. Instead of a large, static object it is effortlessly mobile and even makes a laptop seem bulky by comparison.

But even with its compact size, the iPad still manages to pack a lot of power and functionality into its diminutive body. In this case, small is very definitely beautiful and the range of what you can do with the iPad is considerable:

- Communicate via email, video and text messaging

- Surf the Web wirelessly

- Add an endless number of new 'apps' from the Apple App Store

- Use a range of entertainment tools, covering music, photos, video, books and games

- Do all of your favorite productivity tasks such as word processing, creating spreadsheets or producing presentations

- Organize your life with apps for calendars, address books, notes, reminders and much more

Add to this up to 10 hours' battery life when you are on the move, a Retina Display screen of outstanding clarity and a seamless backup system, and it is clear why the iPad can fulfil all of your computing needs.

Don't forget

The latest version of the iPad is the fourth generation. It comes in either white or black.

Don't forget

'Apps' is just a fancy name for what are more traditionally called programs in the world of computing. The iPad has several apps that come built-in and ready for use. There are thousands more available for downloading from the online App Store (see page 68).

Simplicity of the iPad

Computers have become a central part of our everyday lives, but there is no reason why they need to be complex devices that have us scratching our heads as to how to best use them. The iPad is not only stylish and compact, it also makes the computing process as simple as possible, so you can concentrate on what you want to do. Some ways in which this is done are:

- **Instantly on.** With the iPad there is no long wait for it to turn on, or wake from a state of sleep. When you turn it on, it is ready to use, it's as simple as that

- **Apps.** iPad apps sit on the home screen, visible and ready to use. Most apps are created in a similar format, so once you have mastered getting around them you will be comfortable using most apps

- **Settings.** One of the built-in iPad apps is for Settings. This is a one-stop shop for customizing the way that your iPad looks and operates and also how settings for apps work

Settings

- **Dock and Multitasking Bar.** These are two functions that enable you to quickly access your favorite apps, regardless of what you are doing on your iPad

- **Home button.** This enables you to return to the main home screen at any time. It also has some additional functionality, depending on how many times you click it

The Right Version for You

The iPad is now in its fourth generation. Following the earlier versions, this is now known by just the title iPad. There are two different versions of the full-sized iPad:

- With Wi-Fi connectivity. This enables you to connect to the Internet via a Wi-Fi router, either in your own home, or at a Wi-Fi hotspot

- With Wi-Fi and 4G connectivity (where available, but it also covers 3G)

Each version also has different levels of storage and so the decision as to which one is right for you will largely be based on the following:

- Will you need it to connect to the Internet when you are using it on the move? If not, then the standard model with Wi-Fi should be sufficient

- Will you want to download a lot of music, videos, books and photos on your iPad? The more of these that you use, the more storage you will need. You can monitor the amount of storage that you have used within the Settings>General>Usage>Storage section. This displays the amount of storage used by each app:

General	Usage	
Storage		
7.2 GB Available		6.2 GB Used
Photos & Camera		1.4 GB >
Music		1.1 GB >
Serenity		475 MB >
iMovie		446 MB >
Numbers		343 MB >
Keynote		338 MB >
Pages		287 MB >
iPhoto		136 MB >

Specifications

The specifications for the iPad are:

- **Height:** 9.50 inches (241.2 mm), width: 7.31 inches (185.7 mm), depth: 0.37 inch (9.4 mm)

- **Processor:** Dual-core Apple A6X with quad-core graphics

- **Storage:** 16 GB, 32 GB or 64 GB of in-built flash storage

- **Wireless:** Wi-Fi (802.11a/b/g/n; 802.11n on 2.4 GHz and 5 GHz), Bluetooth 4.0

- **Screen:** Retina Display, 9.7-inch (diagonal) LED-backlit glossy widescreen Multi-Touch display with IPS technology, 2048 by 1536 pixel resolution at 264 pixels per inch (ppi), fingerprint-resistant oleophobic coating

- **Battery power:** Up to 10 hours of surfing the Web on Wi-Fi, watching video, or listening to music

- **Battery charging:** Via power adapter (supplied) or USB to computer system

- **Input/Output:** Lightning connector port, 3.5 mm stereo headphone minijack, built-in speaker, microphone and micro-SIM card tray (Wi-Fi + 4G model only)

- **Sensors:** Accelerometer, ambient light sensor and gyroscope

- **TV and video:** AirPlay Mirroring to Apple TV for viewing content on an HDTV

- **Mail attachment support:** The following file formats can be opened or viewed through the Mail app: .jpg, .tiff, .gif (images); .doc and .docx (Microsoft Word); .htm and .html (web pages); .key (Keynote); .numbers (Numbers); .pages (Pages); .pdf (Preview and Adobe Acrobat); .ppt and .pptx (Microsoft PowerPoint); .txt (text); .rtf (rich text format); .vcf (contact information); .xls and .xlsx (Microsoft Excel)

Beware

Even if you initially think you will not use a lot of storage, this may change once you have bought your iPad. If possible, buy a version with as much storage as possible.

Hot tip

To connect your iPad to an HDTV you will need an Apple Lightning (or Dock) Digital AV Adapter or an Apple Lightning (or Dock) to VGA Adapter (sold separately).

11

Before you Switch On

The external controls for the iPad are simple. Three of them are situated at the top of the iPad and the other is in the middle at the bottom. There are also two cameras, one on the front and one on the back of the iPad.

Controls

The controls at the top of the iPad are:

On/Off button

Side switch for silent mode (this applies to system sounds rather than the volume of items such as music or videos)

Volume Up or Down button

Cameras. One is located on the back, underneath the On/Off button and one on the front, top

Home button. Press this once to wake up the iPad or return to the Home screen at any point:

Speaker. The speaker is located on the bottom of the iPad:

Lightning connector. Connect the Lightning connector here to charge the iPad, or connect it to another computer. (See page 18 for more information on the connector for previous versions of the iPad)

Don't forget

To turn on the iPad, press and hold the On/Off button for a few seconds. It can also be used to Sleep the iPad or Wake it from the Sleep state.

Hot tip

The Side switch can also be used to lock the rotation of the iPad screen. For details see Chapter Two, page 26.

Don't forget

The fourth generation iPad has an iSight camera on the back, which is a 5-megapixel camera which can also capture video in HD.

Getting Started

To start using the iPad, press the On/Off button once and hold it down for a few seconds.

Initially there will be a series of Setup screens to move through before you can use the iPad:

1 Drag this slider (using one finger) to the right to start the Setup process

Hot tip

If your iPad ever freezes, or if something is not working properly, it can be rebooted by holding down the Home button and the On/Off button for 10 seconds and then turning it on again by pressing and holding the Home button.

2 After each step of the Setup process, tap once on this arrow in the top right-hand corner, or the Next button

Beware

Some people are uneasy about revealing their location via their iPad. However, it is a useful function that can be used constructively by a number of apps. If you are uncomfortable about it, it can be disabled.

The Setup process covers the following items:

- **Language.** Select the language you want to use

- **Country.** Select the country in which you are located

- **Location Services.** This determines whether your iPad can use your geographical location for apps that use this type of information (such as Maps)

- **Wi-Fi network.** Select a Wi-Fi network to connect to the Internet. If you are at home, this will be your own Wi-Fi network, if available. If you are at a Wi-Fi hotspot then this will appear on your network list

...cont'd

Don't forget

For details about obtaining an Apple ID see Chapter Five.

Don't forget

For more information about using iCloud see Chapter Two.

Hot tip

The Find My iPad function can also be set up within the Location Services and iCloud sections of the Settings app.

- **Apple ID.** You can register with this to be able to access a range of Apple facilities, such as iCloud, purchase items on iTunes or the App Store, Facetime, Messages and iBooks

- **iCloud.** This is Apple's online service for sharing and backing up content. You have to register for iCloud, with an Apple ID, and once you have done this you can specify which items you want to be made available to other compatible devices via iCloud

- **Find My iPad.** This is a service that can be activated so that you can locate your iPad if it is lost or stolen. This is done via the online iCloud site at www.icloud.com

- **Dictation.** If this is turned on, a microphone icon on the virtual keyboard can be used to enter text by speaking rather than typing

- **Diagnostic information.** This enables information about your iPad to be sent to Apple

- **Register.** This enables you to register your iPad with Apple, as the registered owner

- **Start using.** Once the setup process has been completed you can start using your iPad

Home Screen

Once you have completed the Setup process you will see the Home screen of the iPad. This contains the built-in apps:

Don't forget

Items on the Dock can be removed and new ones can be added. For more details see Chapter Two.

At the bottom of the screen are four apps that appear by default in the Dock area.

Rotate the iPad and the orientation changes automatically.

Home Button

The Home button, located at the bottom, middle on the iPad, can be used to perform a number of tasks:

1 Click once on the Home button to return to the Home screen at any point

2 Double-click on the Home button to access the Multitasking Bar. This is at the bottom of the screen and shows the most recently used and open apps. The rest of the Home screen is grayed out. Tap once on an app to access it

Don't forget

For more information about using the iPad search facility, see Chapter Two.

3 Click once on the Home button when on the Home screen to access the iPad search function

Opening Items

All apps on your iPad can be opened with the minimum of fuss and effort:

1 Tap once on an icon to open the app

2 The app opens at its home screen

3 Click once on the Home button to return to the Home screen

4 Access the Multitasking Bar as shown on the previous page. All open apps are shown here. Tap once on an icon to access that app again

Charging your iPad

The iPad comes with a Lightning connector to USB Cable and a USB Power Adapter. These can be used to charge the iPad:

1 Connect the USB end of the Lightning connector to the Power Adapter

2 Connect the other end of the Lightning connector to the iPad

3 Plug in the Power Adapter

The iPad can also be charged by connecting it with the Lightning connector to another computer. However, this has to be another Mac computer and, if it is a MacBook, it also has to be plugged in for the iPad to charge.

2 Around your iPad

Once you have turned on your iPad you will want to start using it as soon as possible. This chapter shows how to do this with details about settings, navigation, accessibility features, the voice assistant Siri and also registering for and setting up the iCloud service for sharing your content.

iPad Settings

The Settings app is the one that should probably be explored first as it controls settings for the appearance of the iPad and the way it, and its apps, operate. To use the Settings app:

1 Tap once on the Settings app icon

2 The Settings are listed down the left-hand side and the options are shown on the right-hand side

Don't forget

If a Settings option has an On/Off button next to it, this can be changed by swiping the button to either the left or right.

3 Tap on a link to see additional options for that item

4 Tap once here to move back to the main category for the selected Setting

The System Settings are:

- **Airplane Mode.** This can be used while on an airplane

- **Wi-Fi.** This enables you to select a wireless network. Available networks will be displayed here

- **Bluetooth.** Turn this On to connect Bluetooth devices

- **Do Not Disturb.** Use this to specify times when you do not want to receive audio alerts or FaceTime video calls

- **Notifications.** This determines how the Notification Center operates in terms of alerting the user to different types of notifications

- **General.** This contains a number of options for how the iPad operates. This is one of the most useful Settings

- **Sounds.** This contains options for setting sounds for alerts for items such as mail and calendar items

- **Brightness & Wallpaper.** This can be used to set the screen brightness manually or automatically and select a wallpaper

- **Picture Frame.** This can activate your iPad as a picture frame when it is locked

- **Privacy.** This can be used to activate Location Services so that your location can be used by specific apps

- **iCloud.** This contains settings for items that are to be saved to the online iCloud

- **Mail, Contacts, Calendars.** This has options for how these three apps operate

...cont'd

- **Notes.** This contains formatting options for creating items in the Notes app

- **Reminders.** This has an option for syncing your reminders for other devices, covering a period of time

- **Messages.** This can be used to sign in to the Messages app for sending and receiving text messages

- **FaceTime.** This is used to turn video calling On or Off

- **Maps.** This contains options for displaying distances in miles or kilometers in the Maps app and also the way labels are displayed on maps

- **Safari.** Settings for the Safari Web browser

- **iTunes & App Stores.** This can be used to specify downloading options from the iTunes Store and the App Store, for music, books and apps

- **Music.** This has options for how you listen to music

- **Video.** This has options for how you view videos

- **Photos & Camera.** This has options for viewing and editing photos, slideshow settings and options for uploading to iCloud, and using Shared Photo Streams

- **iBooks.** This contains options for reading books in the iBooks app, including hyphenation and using bookmarks

- **Newsstand.** Use this set of options to automatically download new content for items in the Newsstand app

- **Twitter.** Use this to install Twitter and create an account

- **Facebook.** As above, but for Facebook

Beware

If you turn on Private Browsing within the Safari Settings, no record of visited Web pages will be kept.

Hot tip

Within a number of apps there is a Share button that can be used to share items through a variety of methods, including email, Facebook and Twitter. To access these, tap once on this button, if available.

Using the Dock

By default, there are four apps on the Dock, at the bottom of the screen. These are the four that Apple thinks you will use most frequently:

- Safari, for Web browsing
- Mail, for email
- Videos
- Music

You can rearrange the order in which the Dock apps appear:

1 Tap and hold on one of the Dock apps until it starts to jiggle

2 Drag the app into its new position

3 Click once on the Home button to return from edit mode

Hot tip

Just above the Dock is a small magnifying glass icon and a number of small dots. The magnifying glass can be used to access the Search function, by tapping on it once. The dots indicate how many screens of content there are on the iPad. Tap on one of the dots to go to that screen.

...cont'd

Adding and removing Dock apps

You can also remove apps from the Dock and add new ones:

1   To remove an app from the Dock tap and hold it and drag it onto the main screen area

Don't forget

If items are removed from the Dock they are still available in the same way from the main screen.

2   To add an app to the Dock tap and hold it and drag it onto the Dock

3   The number of items that can be added to the Dock is restricted to a maximum of six as the icons do not resize themselves

4   Click once on the Home button to return from edit mode

Multitasking Bar

The Multitasking Bar can be accessed at the bottom of the screen and it performs a number of tasks:

- It shows open apps

- It allows access to music and video controls

- It allows screen rotation to be locked

- It enables apps to be closed

Accessing the Multitasking Bar

The Multitasking Bar can be accessed in two ways:

1   Double-click on the Home button

2   Swipe up, from the bottom of the screen, with four or five fingers

Don't forget

The Multitasking Bar can be accessed from either the Home screen or any open app. To exit the Multitasking Bar, tap once on the main screen, or click once on the Home button to return to the Home screen.

3   Swipe left and right to view the items on the Multitasking Bar

...cont'd

Accessing Controls

To access the music and video controls:

 1 Swipe from left to right on the Multitasking Bar

 2 Use the controls to, from left to right, rewind a song or video, play a song or video, fast forward a song or video, adjust the volume of a song or video

Locking screen rotation

The Multitasking Bar can also be used to lock the screen rotation so that the orientation stays the same regardless of how you move the iPad. To do this:

1 Swipe from left to right on the Multitasking Bar

2 Tap once on this icon

3 The padlock icon indicates that the screen rotation is locked

---

Hot tip

The screen rotation can also be locked from within the General section of the Settings app. Under 'Use Side Switch to:', tap once on the Lock Rotation link. Then the side switch can be used to lock, and unlock, the screen rotation. If this is selected, the button in Step 2 can be used to mute the system volume instead.

Closing Items

The iPad deals with open apps very efficiently. They do not interact with other apps, which increases security and also means that they can be open in the background, without using up a significant amount of processing power, in a state of semi-hibernation until they are needed. Because of this it is not essential to close apps when you move to something else. However, you may want to do this to clear up the Multitasking Bar, or if an app stops working. To do this:

1. Access the Multitasking Bar. Tap and hold on an app until the icon starts to jiggle and a red circle appears in the left-hand corner

Don't forget

When you switch from one app to another, the first one stays open in the background. You can go back to it by accessing it from the Multitasking Bar or the Home screen.

27

2. Tap once on the red circle to close the app

3. The app is removed from the Multitasking Bar

4. The app is only closed, not removed from your iPad. It is still accessible from the Home screen and when you open it again it will be available on the Multitasking Bar too

Navigating Around

Most of the navigation on the iPad is done with Multi-Touch Gestures, which are looked at on the next three pages. Two of these can also be used for basic navigation:

Swiping between screens

Once you have added more apps to your iPad they will start to fill up more screens. To move between these:

Swipe left or right with one, or two, fingers.

Returning to the Home screen

Pinch together with thumb and four fingers to return to the Home screen from any open app.

Swipe, Tap and Pinch

Since there is no mouse connected to the iPad, navigation is done with your fingers. There is a combination of tapping, swiping and pinching gestures that can be used to view items such as Web pages, photos, maps and documents and also navigate around the iPad.

Swiping up and down

Swipe up and down with one finger to move up or down Web pages, photos, maps or documents. The content moves in the opposite direction of the swipe, i.e. if you swipe up, the page will move down and vice versa.

Hot tip

The faster you swipe on the screen, the faster the screen moves up or down.

Tapping and zooming

Double-tap with one finger to zoom in on a Web page, photo, map or document. Double-tap with two fingers to return to the original view.

...cont'd

Pinching and swiping

Swipe outwards with thumb and forefinger to zoom in on a Web page, photo, map or document.

Pinch together with thumb and forefinger to zoom back out on a Web page, photo, map or document.

More gestures

- Swipe left or right with four or five fingers to move between open apps

- Swipe up with four or five fingers to reveal the Multitasking Bar at the bottom of the screen

- Drag with two or three fingers to move a Web page, photo, map or document

- Swipe left or right with one finger to move between full-size photos in the Photos app

- Tap once on a photo thumbnail with one finger to enlarge it to full screen within the Photos app

- Tap once with two fingers on a full-size photo to reduce it to a thumbnail within the Photos app

- Drag down at the top-middle of the iPad to view current notifications in the Notification Center

Hot tip

The gestures involving four or five fingers can be turned On or Off in the General section of the Settings app.

Searching with Spotlight

Spotlight is the search facility that is provided with the iPad. It can be accessed from the main Home screen by clicking once on the Home button.

Spotlight can search for apps on your iPad and also search for items within the following apps:

● Calendar

● Contacts

● Mail

● Messages

● Music, video, podcasts and audiobooks

● Notes and events

● Reminders

To search for items with Spotlight:

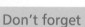

Don't forget

To return to the Home screen from the Search page, click once on the Home button.

1 Type the search keywords into the search box

2 Tap once on one of the results

3 Tap once on these buttons to search for the item over the Web or Wikipedia

Launching apps with Spotlight

Once you have downloaded a lot of apps, and they are on several screens, Spotlight can be a good way to quickly find and launch specific apps. To do this:

1 Enter the name, or part of it, of the app into the search box

2 Tap once on the app name to launch it

Spotlight settings

Within the Settings app you can select which items the Spotlight search operates over. To do this:

1 Tap once on the Settings app

2 Tap once on General tab

3 Tap once on the Spotlight Search link

4 Tap once on an item to exclude it from the Spotlight search

Finding Things with Siri

Siri is the iPad voice assistant that provides answers to a variety of questions by looking at your iPad and also Web services. You can ask Siri questions relating to the apps on your iPad and also general questions, such as weather conditions around the world, or sports results. Initially, Siri can be set up within the Settings app:

1 In the General section, tap once on this link

2 Drag the Siri button to On to activate the Siri functionality. Tap once on these links to select a language, set voice feedback and allow access to your details

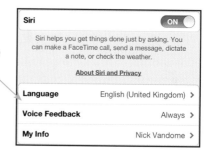

Questioning Siri

Once you have set up Siri, you can start putting it to work with your queries. To do this:

1 Hold down the Home button until the Siri window appears

2 To find something from your iPad apps, ask a question such as, 'Show me my reminders'

Hot tip

Using explicit language with Siri can be blocked within Restrictions in the General section of the Settings app. See Chapter 12 for more details about setting restrictions.

Hot tip

Siri can be used to open any of the built-in iPad apps, simply by saying, 'Open Photos'.

Siri can also find information from across the Web and related Web services:

① Siri can provide sports results, for certain sports in certain countries, such as in response to the question, 'How did the Red Sox get on in their last match?'

35

② Weather reports are another of Siri's strong points and it even adds in a bit of editorial comment in response to the question, 'What is the weather like in Mexico City?'

③ However, even Siri's knowledge is limited and if there is a subject it does not recognize it will own up and offer to search the Web instead

Accessibility Issues

The iPad tries to cater to as wide a range of users as possible, including those who have difficulty with vision, hearing or physical and motor issues. There are a number of settings that can help with these areas. To access the range of accessibility settings:

Don't forget

You may have to scroll down the page to view and access the Accessibility link.

1 Tap once on the Settings app

2 Tap once on the General tab

3 Tap once on the Accessibility link

Accessibility ›

Beware

VoiceOver works with the built-in iPad apps and some apps from the App Store, but not all of them.

4 The settings for Vision, Hearing and Physical & Motor are displayed here

Vision settings

These can help anyone with impaired vision and there are options to hear items on the screen and also for making text easier to read:

1 Tap once on the VoiceOver link

| VoiceOver | Off > |

Don't forget

When VoiceOver is On, tap once on an item to select it and have it spoken; double-tap to activate the item.

2 Drag this button to On to activate the VoiceOver function. This then enables items to be spoken when you tap on them

VoiceOver   ON

VoiceOver speaks items on the screen:
• Tap once to select an item
• Double-Tap to activate the selected item
• Swipe three fingers to scroll

VoiceOver Practice

3 Select options for VoiceOver as required

Speak Hints	ON
Speaking Rate	
Typing Feedback	>
Use Phonetics	ON
Use Pitch Change	ON
Use Compact Voice	OFF

Hot tip

There is a wide range of options for the way VoiceOver can be used. For full details see the Apple website at www.apple.com/accessibility/ipad/vision.htm

37

...cont'd

Don't forget

If you turn on the Zoom function you can magnify the whole screen by double-tapping twice. To move around the screen, drag with three fingers. To change the amount of zoom, double-tap with three fingers and drag up or down on the screen.

Hot tip

The Speak Auto-text function can be turned on so that auto-corrections and auto-capitalizations are automatically spoken.

4 Tap once on the Accessibility button to return to the main options

5 Tap once on these buttons to access options for zooming the screen, increasing text size, inverting the text color on the screen and speaking text options

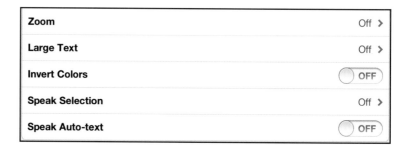

Zoom	Off >
Large Text	Off >
Invert Colors	OFF
Speak Selection	Off >
Speak Auto-text	OFF

6 Tap once on the Accessibility button to return to the main options after each selection

Hearing settings

These can be used to change the iPad speaker from stereo to mono. To do this:

1 Drag this button to On to enable Mono Audio

Hearing

Mono Audio ON

L ━━━━━●━━━━━ R

2 Drag this button to specify whether sound comes out of the left or the right side of the speaker

AssistiveTouch

This can be used by anyone who has difficulty navigating around the iPad with the screen or buttons. It can be used with an external device such as a joystick, or it can be used on its own. To use AssistiveTouch:

1 Tap once on the AssistiveTouch link

2 Drag this button to On to activate the AssistiveTouch function

Don't forget

The AssistiveTouch options make it easier for anyone with difficulties clicking the Home button, or using Multi-Touch Gestures.

3 The AssistiveTouch icon appears on the screen and can be dragged around

4 Tap once on the AssistiveTouch icon to view its options

5 Tap once on the Home icon to return to the Home screen

...cont'd

6 Tap once on the Favorites icon to access options for using custom gestures

7 To create a custom gesture, tap once on this link under the AsssitiveTouch section

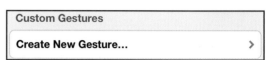

8 Drag on the screen with the required gesture (e.g. pinching inwards with thumb and four fingers to access the Home screen)

Don't forget

The Gestures section can be used to perform Multi-Touch Gestures, without having to physically use the full number of fingers on the screen.

9 Tap once on the Save button

10 Give the gesture a name and tap once on the Save button

Hot tip

The Favorites section can also be used to create custom gestures. To do this, tap once on one of the empty boxes and then record the gesture in the New Gesture window. Once it is saved it becomes available in the Favorites section.

11 The gesture is added under the Favorites section

12 Tap once on a gesture to select it. The corresponding number of blue circles appear on the screen. Tap once on one of the circles to perform the action associated with the gesture

13 Tap once on the Device icon

14 Tap once to activate the required function, including changing the screen rotation and adjusting the volume

Triple-click options

The Home button can also be used with a triple-click action to perform a variety of accessibility tasks. To do this:

1 Tap once on the Triple-click Home link

Triple-click Home	Off >

2 Tap once on one of these options to set this as the action for when you triple-click the Home button

Triple-click the Home Button for:	
VoiceOver	
Invert Colors	✓
Zoom	
AssistiveTouch	

...cont'd

Guided Access

The Guided Access option allows for certain functionality within an app to be disabled so that individual tasks can be focused on without any other distractions. To use this:

1 Under the Learning heading tap once on the Guided Access link

2 Drag this button to On to activate the Guided Access functionality

3 Open an app and triple-click on the Home button to activate Guided Access

4 Drag this button to Off if you want to disable the touch function within the app

5 Circle an area on the screen to disable it (this can be any functionality within the app

6 Tap once on the Start button to begin using the app in Guided Access mode

Auto-Locking the Screen

To save power it is possible to set your iPad screen to auto-lock. This is the equivalent of the sleep option on a traditional computer. To do this:

1 Tap once on the Settings app

2 Tap once on the General tab

3 Tap once on the Auto-Lock link

Auto-Lock	Never >

4 Tap once on a duration for when the screen is locked

5 Once the screen is locked, drag this button to the right to unlock the screen

Don't forget

The screen can also be locked by clicking once on the On/Off button at the top of the iPad.

Don't forget

Auto-locking the screen does not prevent other people from accessing your iPad. If you want to prevent anyone else having access, it can be locked with a passcode. See Chapter 12 for details.

Updating Software

The operating system that powers the iPad is known as iOS. This is a mobile computing operating system and it is also used on the iPhone and the iPod Touch. The latest version is iOS 6. Periodically, there are updates to the iOS, to fix bugs and add new features. These can be downloaded to your iPad once they are released:

1 Tap once on the Settings app

2 Tap once on the General tab

3 Tap once on the Software Update link

Software Update   >

4 If there is an update available it will be displayed here, with details of what is contained within it

5 Tap once on this button to download and install the iOS update. This will then be done automatically

44

Living in the iCloud

iCloud is the Apple online service that performs a number of valuable functions:

- It makes your content available across multiple devices. The content is stored in the iCloud and then pushed out to other iCloud-enabled devices, including the iPhone, iPod Touch and other Mac or Windows computers

- It enables online access to your content via the iCloud website. This includes your iCloud email, contacts, calendar and reminders

- It backs up the content on your iPad

Once you have registered for and set up iCloud, it works automatically so you do not have to worry about anything. You can activate iCloud when you first set up your iPad, or:

1 Tap once on the Settings app

2 Tap once on the iCloud tab

3 Tap once on the Account link

4 Enter your Apple ID and password to set up iCloud on your iPad

Don't forget

It is free to register and set up a standard iCloud account.

Hot tip

To access your iCloud account through the website, access www.icloud.com and enter your Apple ID details.

...cont'd

Don't forget

The Account window also has details of your iCloud email account.

Beware

By default, you get 5 GB of free storage space with an iCloud account. However, there is an introductory offer until a certain date. Make sure you select the Downgrade Options and choose the Free Plan to ensure you do not automatically get put onto a paid-for storage Plan.

Don't forget

The Apple iWork apps, Pages, Keynote and Numbers, have their content saved into the iCloud under Documents & Data.

5 Tap once here to view your current storage details

6 Upgrade options are displayed. Tap once on this button and then select the free 5 GB storage option

iCloud settings

Once you have set up your iCloud account you can then apply settings for how it works. Once you have done this you will not have to worry about it again:

1 Access the iCloud section in the Settings app, as above

2 Drag these buttons to On for each item that you wish to be included in iCloud. Each item is then saved and stored in the iCloud and made available to your other iCloud-enabled devices

3 Tap once on the Photo Stream and Documents & Data links to access the buttons for turning these On

iCloud Storage & Backup

It is possible to view how the storage on your iCloud account is being used and also specify how your content is backed up to iCloud. To do this:

1 Access the iCloud section in the Settings app, as above, and tap once on the Storage & Backup link

2 Tap once on the Manage Storage link to view how your iCloud storage is being used

3 Tap once on an app to view the individual documents within it that are being stored

Don't forget

Tap once on the Back Up Now button at Step 4 to perform a manual backup of your iPad content.

4 Drag this button to On to enable automatic backups

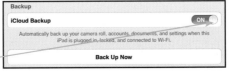

iPad Smart Cover

To prevent the iPad screen getting scratched, a cover (known as a Smart Cover) can be used as protection. This can also be used as a stand to support the iPad for viewing content or typing with the keyboard.

There are settings for the iPad cover in the Settings app. This can enable it to lock or unlock the iPad:

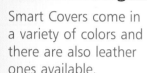
1 Tap once on the Settings app

2 Tap once on the General tab

3 Under iPad Cover Lock/Unlock drag the button

iPad Cover Lock / Unlock   ON

to On to enable the cover to lock or unlock the iPad when it is placed in position or removed

Attaching the cover

The iPad cover attaches with a hinge along the left-hand side of the iPad. Attach it by placing the hinge on the side of the iPad until it clicks magnetically into place.

Using the cover as a stand

The iPad cover is separated into four foldable panels. These can be folded into a triangular shape to create a stand for the iPad:

3 The iPad Keyboard

The iPad has a virtual keyboard rather than a traditional one. This chapter shows how to use it and also edit text and add shortcuts.

It's Virtually a Keyboard

The keyboard on the iPad is a virtual one, i.e. it appears on the touch screen whenever text or numbered input is required for an app. This can be for a variety of reasons:

- Entering text with a word processing app, email or an organizing app such as Notes

- Entering a Web address in a Web browser such as the Safari app

- Entering information into a form

- Entering a password

Viewing the keyboard

When you attempt one of the items above, the keyboard appears so that you can enter any text or numbers:

Around the keyboard

To access the various keyboard controls:

1   Tap once on this button to create a Cap text letter

2   Double-tap on this button to create Caps Lock

3   Tap once on this button to back delete an item

4 Tap once on this button to access the Numbers keyboard option

5 From the Numbers keyboard, tap once on this button to access the Symbols keyboard

6 Tap once on this button on either of the two keyboards above to return to the standard QWERTY option

ABC

7 Tap once on this button to hide the keyboard (this can be done from any of the keyboard options). If the keyboard is hidden, tap once on one of the input options, e.g. entering text, to show it again

Keyboard Settings

Settings for the keyboard can be determined in the General section of the Settings app. To do this:

1   Tap once on the Settings app

2   Tap once on the General tab

3   Tap once on the Keyboard link

Keyboard	>

4   Drag this slider to On to enable Auto-Capitalization, i.e. letters will automatically be capitalized at the beginning of a sentence

Auto-Capitalization	ON

Hot tip

The Auto-Correction function works as you type a word, so it may change a number of times, depending on the length of the word you are typing.

5   Drag this slider to On to enable Auto-Correction, i.e. suggestions for words will appear as you type, particularly if you have mis-typed a word

Auto-Correction	ON

6   Drag this slider to On to check spelling as you type

Check Spelling	ON

7 Drag this slider to On to enable the Caps Lock function to be performed

Enable Caps Lock	ON

8 Drag this slider to On to enable shortcut functionality

"." Shortcut	ON

Don't forget

For more information about keyboard shortcuts, see pages 59–61.

9 Drag this slider to On to enable the keyboard to be split and moved. Tap once on the Keyboards link to access options for adding different international keyboards

Keyboards	1 >
Split Keyboard	ON

10 Tap once on this link to view existing text shortcuts and also to create new ones

Shortcuts	
omw	On my way! >
Add New Shortcut...	>

11 Tap once on this link to create new shortcuts

Entering Text

Once you have applied the keyboard settings that you require you can start entering text. To do this:

1 Tap once on the screen to activate the keyboard. Start typing with the keyboard. The text will appear at the point where you tapped on the screen

2 As you type, Auto-Correction comes up with suggestions. Tap once on the spacebar to accept the suggestion, or tap once on the cross next to it to reject it

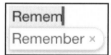

3 If Check Spelling is enabled, any misspelled words appear underlined in red

Remember to go to the supermrket

4 Tap once on this button to hide the keyboard

Editing Text

Once text has been entered it can be selected, copied, cut and pasted. Depending on the app being used, the text can also be formatted, such as with a word processing app.

Selecting text
To select text and perform tasks on it:

1 To change the insertion point, tap and hold until the magnifying glass appears

2 Drag the magnifying glass to move the insertion point

3 Tap once at the insertion point to access the selection buttons

4 Double-tap on a word to select it. Tap once on Cut or Copy as required

5 Drag the selection handles to expand or contract the selection

6 If text has been copied, tap and hold at a new point on the page and tap once on Paste

Hot tip

Once the selection buttons have been accessed, tap once on Select to select the previous word, or Select All to select all of the text.

...cont'd

Formatting text

Once text has been added to a document it can be formatted in a number of ways (depending on the app). To do this:

1 Select text in a document as shown on the previous page. Instead of copying it, it can be formatted with buttons within the app (this is for the Pages app)

Don't forget

Some apps that allow text entry have formatting options, while others do not and text is just entered in a standard format.

2 Tap once on these buttons to, from left to right, change the font, decrease the font size, set a specific font size and increase the font size

3 Tap once on these buttons to, from left to right, create bold, italic or underlined text or set the text alignment

Moving the Keyboard

By default, the keyboard appears as a single unit along the bottom of the screen. However, it is possible to split the keyboard so that it appears on separate sides of the screen. It is also possible to undock the keyboard and move it around the screen.

Undocking the keyboard

To undock the keyboard from its position at the bottom of the screen:

1 Press and hold on this button on the keyboard

2 Tap once on the Undock button

3 The keyboard is undocked from the bottom of the screen

Hot tip

To redock the keyboard, tap and hold on the button in Step 1 and tap once on the Dock button.

4 Tap and hold here at the side of the button to move the keyboard

5 The keyboard can then be moved to different positions around the screen

...cont'd

Splitting the keyboard

The keyboard can also be split into two and used on either side of the screen. To do this:

 Press and hold on this button on the keyboard

 Tap once on the Split button

 The keyboard is split to the left and the right sides of the screen

 Tap and hold here at the side of the button to move the split keyboard

 Tap and hold on the button above and tap once on the Dock and Merge button to return the keyboard to its default position at the bottom of the screen

Keyboard Shortcuts

There are two types of shortcuts that can be used on the iPad keyboard:

- Shortcuts on the keys on the keyboard

- Shortcuts created with text abbreviations

Shortcuts with keys

The shortcuts that can be created with the keys on the keyboard are:

1 Double-tap on the spacebar to add a full stop/period and a space at the end of a sentence

Hot tip

The shortcut in Step 1 can be disabled by switching off the Shortcut option within the Settings>General> Keyboard section.

2 Swipe up once on the comma (or press and hold) to insert an apostrophe

3 Swipe up once on the full stop/period to insert quotation marks

4 Press and hold on appropriate letters to access accented versions for different languages

...cont'd

Text abbreviations

To create shortcuts with text abbreviations:

1 Tap once on the Settings app

2 Tap once on the General tab

3 Tap once on the Keyboard link

4 Tap once on the Add New Shortcut... link

5 Enter the phrase you want to be made into a shortcut

6 Enter the abbreviation you want to use as the shortcut for the phrase

7 Tap once on the Save button

8 The shortcut is displayed here

Using shortcuts

Once you have created shortcuts you can then use them with the iPad keyboard. To do this:

1 Enter the abbreviation. As you type, the phrase appears underneath the abbreviation

2 Tap once on the spacebar to add the phrase, or tap once on the cross to reject it

Deleting shortcuts

Shortcuts can be deleted, if you do not want to use them anymore. To do this:

1 In the Keyboard section of the General Settings, tap once on the Edit button

Edit

2 Tap once on the red circle next to the shortcut you want to delete

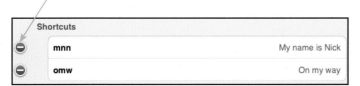

Shortcuts	
mnn	My name is Nick
omw	On my way

3 Tap once on the Delete button to remove the shortcut

4 Tap once on the Done button

Done

61

Dictation

On the keyboard there is also a dictation option, which enables you to enter text by speaking into a microphone, rather than typing on the keyboard. This is On by default.

Using dictation

Dictation can be used with any app with a text input function. To do this:

1 Tap once on this button on the keyboard to activate the dictation microphone. Speak into the microphone to record text

2 Tap once on the microphone button again to finish the recording

3 As the dictation function is processing the recording these buttons appear

4 Once the recording has been processed the text appears in the app

4 Knowing your Apps

Apps are the parts that keep the iPad engine running. This chapter details the built-in ones and also shows how to access and use apps from the App Store.

What is an App?

An app is just a more modern name for a computer program. Initially, it was used in relation to mobile devices, such as the iPhone and the iPad, but it is now becoming more widely used with desktop and laptop computers, for both Mac and Windows operating systems.

On the iPad there are two types of apps:

- **Built-in apps.** These are the apps that come pre-installed on the iPad

- **App Store apps.**
These are apps that can be downloaded from the online App Store. There is a huge range of apps available here, covering a variety of different categories. Some are free while others have to be paid for. The apps here are updated and added to on a daily basis so there are always new ones to explore

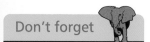

Don't forget

You need an active Internet connection to download apps from the App Store.

64

There are also two important points about apps (both built-in and those from the App Store) to remember:

- Apart from some of the built-in apps, the majority of apps do not interact with each other. This means that there is less chance of viruses being transmitted from app to app on your iPad and they can operate without a reliance on other apps

- Content created by apps is saved within the app itself, rather than within a file structure on your iPad, e.g. if you create a note in the Notes app, it is saved here, if you take a photo, it is saved in the Photos app. Content is usually also saved automatically when it is created, or edited, so you do not have to worry about saving it as you work on it

Built-in Apps

The built-in iPad apps are the ones that appear on the Home screen when you turn on the iPad:

Don't forget

The iPad Settings app is another of the built-in apps and this is looked at in detail in Chapter Two.

- **App Store.** This can be used to access the App Store, from where additional apps can then be downloaded

Don't forget

Some of the built-in apps, such as Mail and Contacts, interact with each other. However, since these are designed by Apple there is almost no chance of them containing viruses.

- **Calendar.** An app for storing appointments, important dates and other calendar information. It can be synced with iCloud

- **Clock.** This can be used to view the time in different countries and also as an alarm clock and a stopwatch

- **Contacts.** An address book app. Once contacts are added here they can then also be accessed from other apps, such as Mail

- **FaceTime.** This is an app that uses the built-in FaceTime camera on the iPad to hold video chat with other iPad users, or those with an iPhone, iPod Touch or a Mac computer

...cont'd

● **Game Center.** For those who like gaming, this is an app for playing a variety of games, either individually or with friends

● **iBooks.** This is an app for downloading electronic books, that can then be read on the iPad. This can be done for plain text or illustrated iBooks. Although this is considered a built-in app, it has to first be downloaded from the App Store

● **iTunes.** This app can be used to browse the iTunes store where music, TV shows, movies and more, can be dowloaded to your iPad

● **Mail.** This is the email app for sending and receiving email on your iPad

● **Maps.** Use this app to view maps from around the world, find specific locations and get directions to destinations

● **Messages.** This is the iPad messaging service, which can be used between iPads, iPhones, iPod Touches and Mac computers. It can be used with not only text but also photos and videos

- **Music.** An app for playing music on your iPad and also viewing cover artwork. You can also use it to create your own playlists

- **Newsstand.** Similar to iBooks, this app can be used to download and read newspaper and magazines

Hot tip

It is worth investing in a good pair of headphones for listening to music so you don't disturb other people.

- **Notes.** If you need to jot down your thoughts or ideas, this app is perfect for just that

- **Photo Booth.** A photography app that can be used to create distorted and special effects photos of people or objects

- **Photos.** This is an app for viewing and editing photos and creating slideshows

- **Reminders.** Use this app for organization, when you want to create to-do lists and set reminders for events

- **Safari.** The Apple Web browser that has been developed for viewing the Web on your iPad

- **Video.** This is an app for viewing videos on your iPad and also streaming them to a larger HDTV monitor

About the App Store

While the built-in apps that come with the iPad are flexible and versatile, it really comes into its own when you connect to the App Store. This is an online resource and there are thousands of apps here that can be downloaded and then used on your iPad, including categories from Lifestyle to Travel and Medical.

To use the App Store, you must first have an Apple ID. This can be obtained when you first connect to the App Store. Once you have an Apple ID you can start exploring the App Store:

Don't forget

For full details about obtaining an Apple ID, see Chapter Five.

68

1 Tap once on the App Store icon on the Home screen

2 The latest available apps are displayed on the homepage of the App Store, including the Editor's Choice, featured in the top panel

Don't forget

The Genius function is created within the App Store to highlight similar apps to the ones you have downloaded.

3 Tap on these buttons to view the apps according to Featured, Charts, Genius and Purchased

Viewing apps

To view apps in the App Store and read about their content and functionality:

1 Tap once on an app

2 General details about the app are displayed

Don't forget

If it is an upgraded version of an app, this page will include details of any fixes and improvements that have been made.

3 Swipe left or right here to view additional information about the app and view details

4 Ratings and reviews are available from the relevant button, next to the Details button

Finding Apps

Featured

Within the App Store, apps are separated into categories according to type. This enables you to find apps according to particular subjects. To do this:

1. Tap once on the Featured button on the toolbar at the bottom of the App Store

2. Scroll left and right to view different category headings

Don't forget

Some apps will differ depending on the geographical location from where you are accessing the App Store.

3. Scroll up the page to view additional categories and Quick Links

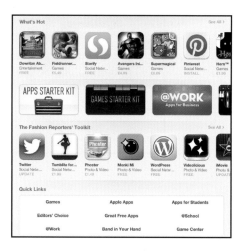

4. Use these buttons at the top of the window to refine the categories for looking for apps

...cont'd

Charts

To find the top rating apps:

1 Tap once on the Charts button on the toolbar at the bottom of the App Store

2 The top overall paid for, free and top grossing apps are displayed

Beware

Do not limit yourself to just viewing the top apps. Although these are the most popular, there are also a lot of excellent apps within each category.

71

3 To find the top apps in different categories, tap once on this button

4 Tap once on a category

5 The top apps for that category are displayed

...cont'd

Genius

This is a feature which suggests similar apps to those you have already downloaded. To use this:

1 Tap once on the Genius button on the toolbar at the bottom of the App Store

2 Tap once on the Turn On Genius button

3 Enter your Apple ID details

4 Agree to the Terms and Conditions

5 Tap once on the Done button

6 Relevant recommendations will appear in the Genius window once you have started downloading apps, based on your previous selections

Searching for apps

Another way to find apps is with the App Store Search box, which is located at the top-right corner of the App Store window. To use this:

1 Tap once in the Search box to bring up the iPad virtual keyboard

Don't forget

For more information about using the iPad virtual keyboard see Chapter Three.

2 Enter a search keyword or phrase

3 Suggested apps appear as you are typing

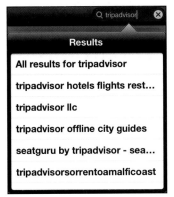

4 Tap once on an app to view it

73

Downloading Apps

When you identify an app that you would like to use, it can be downloaded to your iPad. To do this:

Don't forget

Apps usually download in a few minutes, or less, depending on the speed of your Wi-Fi connection.

Beware

Some apps have 'in-app purchases'. This is additional content that has to be paid for when it is downloaded.

1 Find the app you want to download and tap once on the button next to the app (this will say Free or will have a price)

2 The button changes to say Install. Tap on this once

3 Enter your Apple ID details and tap once on the OK button

4 The app will begin to download on your iPad

5 Once the app is downloaded tap once on it to open and use it (the most recently-downloaded apps have a 'New' label on their icons)

Updating Apps

The world of apps is a dynamic and fast-moving one and new apps are being created and added to the App Store on a daily basis. Existing apps are also being updated, to improve their performance and functionality. Once you have installed an app from the App Store it is possible to obtain updates, at no extra cost (if the app was paid for). To do this:

1 When an update is available it is denoted by a red icon on the App Store button, showing how many updates are available

Hot tip

You should keep your apps as up-to-date as possible to take advantage of software fixes and any updates to the iPad operating system (iOS).

2 Tap once on the App Store button

3 In the App Store, tap once on the Updates button

4 The available updates are displayed

5 Tap once on the button next to an app to update it

6 Tap once on the Update All button to update all of the required apps

75

Organizing Apps

When you start downloading apps you will probably soon find that you have dozens, if not hundreds, of them. You can move between screens to view all of your apps by swiping left or right with one finger.

To move an app between screens, tap and hold on it until it starts to jiggle and a cross appears in the corner. Then drag it to the side of the screen. If there is space on the next screen the app will be moved here.

As more apps are added it can become hard to find the apps you want, particularly if you have to swipe between several screens. However, it is possible to organize apps into individual folders to make using them more manageable. To do this:

1 Press on an app until it starts to jiggle and a white cross appears at the top-left corner

2 Drag the app over another one

3 A folder is created,
containing the two apps

4 The folder is given a default name,
usually based on the category of
the apps

5 Tap on the folder name and
type a new name if required

6 Click the Home button once
to finish creating the folder

7 Click the Home button again to return to the Home
screen (this is done whenever you want to return to
the Home screen from an apps folder)

8 The folder is added on the Home
screen. Tap once on this to access the
items within it

Deleting Apps

If you decide that you do not want certain apps anymore, they can be deleted from your iPad. However, they remain in the iCloud so that you can reinstall them if you change your mind. This also means that if you delete an app by mistake you can get it back from the App Store without having to pay for it again. To do this:

Beware

If you delete an app it will also delete any data that has been compiled with that app, even if you reinstall it from the App Store.

Don't forget

You cannot delete any of the built-in iPad apps, even by mistake.

1 Press on an app until it starts to jiggle and a white cross appears at the top-left corner

2 Tap once on the white cross to delete the app. In the Delete dialog box, tap once on the Delete button

3 Tap once on the App Store button

4 Tap once on the Purchased button

5 Apps that have been deleted have this iCloud icon next to them

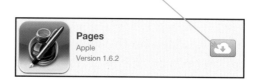

6 Tap once on the iCloud button to reinstall an app

5 Keeping in Touch

We live in a world of varied and instant communications. This chapter shows how to use your iPad to keep ahead in this fast-moving world.

Getting Online

iPads can be used for a variety of different communications, but they all require online access. This is done via Wi-Fi and you will need to have an Internet Service Provider and a Wi-Fi router to connect to the Internet. Once this is in place you will be able to connect to a Wi-Fi network:

1 Tap once on this icon

2 Tap once on the Wi-Fi link

3 Ensure the Wi-Fi button is in the On position

4 Available networks are shown here. Tap once on one to select it

5 Enter a password for your Wi-Fi router

6 Tap once on the Join button

7 Once a network has been joined, a tick appears next to it. This now provides access to the Internet

Don't forget

If you have the 4G version of the iPad you can obtain Internet access this way, but this has to be done through a provider of this service, as with a cell/mobile phone.

Don't forget

If you are connecting to your home Wi-Fi network the iPad should connect automatically each time, after it has been set up. If you are connecting in a public Wi-Fi area you will be asked which network you would like to join.

Obtaining an Apple ID

An Apple ID is a registered email address and password with Apple that enables you to log in and use a variety of online Apple services. These include:

- App Store
- iTunes Store
- iCloud
- iMessage
- FaceTime
- Game Center
- iBooks

It is free to register for an Apple ID and this can be done when you access one of the apps or services which requires this, or you can do it on the Apple website at My Apple ID:

1 Tap once on the Create an Apple ID button

Create an Apple ID

2 Enter your email address and a password

Create an Apple ID.

Choose an Apple ID and password.
Enter your primary email address as your Apple ID. This will be used as the contact email address for your account. Please note that this email address must be verified before you can use certain Apple services.

Apple ID   @mac.com

Password   ••••••••

Confirm Password   ••••••••

Create a security question.
Select a security question or create one of your own. This question will help us verify your identity should you forget your password.

3 Enter additional details such as date of birth and address. Enter the security code and tap once on the Create Apple ID button

Please type the characters you see in the image below.

Try a different image
Vision Impaired

QCTGR

QCTGR
Letters are not case sensitive.

☑ I have read and agree to the Apple Terms of Service and Apple Customer Privacy Policy .

Cancel   Create Apple ID

Setting up an Email Account

Email accounts

Email settings can be specified within the Settings app. Different email accounts can also be added here.

1 Tap once on the Settings app

2 Tap once on the Mail, Contacts, Calendars link

3 Tap once on the Add Account link to add a new account

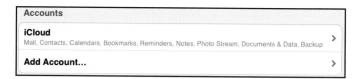

4 Tap once on the type of email account you want to add

Hot tip

If your email provider is not on the Add Account list, tap once on Other at the bottom of the list and complete the account details using the information from your email provider.

5 Enter the details for the account. Tap once on the Next button

6 Drag these buttons On or Off to specify which functions are to be available for the required account

7 Each new account is added under the Accounts heading of the Mail, Contacts, Calendars section

If you set up more than one email account, messages from all of them can be downloaded and displayed by Mail.

Email settings

Email settings can be specified within the Settings app. Different email accounts can also be added here.

1 Under the Mail section there are several options for how Mail operates and looks. These include the number of messages being displayed, previewing emails and font size

Emailing

Email on the iPad is created, sent and received using the Mail app. This provides a range of functionality for managing email, including adding mailboxes and viewing email conversation threads.

Accessing Mail

To access Mail and start sending and receiving emails:

1 Tap once on this icon (the red icon in the corner displays the number of unread emails in your Inbox)

2 Tap once on a message to display it in the main panel

3 Use these buttons to, from left to right, flag a message, move a message, delete a message, respond to a message and create a new message

4 Tap once on this button to reply to a message, forward it to a new recipient, save an image in a message or print it

Hot tip

Images in an email can also be saved by tapping and holding on them and then tapping once on the Save Image button.

Creating email

To create and send an email:

1 Tap once on this button to create a new message

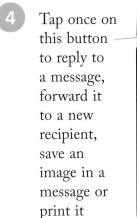

Hot tip

If the recipient is included in your Contacts app, their details will appear as you type. Tap once on the email address, if it appears, to include it in the To field.

2 Enter a recipient name here

To: eilidh

Eildih Vandome
home   eilidhvandome @mac.com

3 Enter a subject

Subject: **Lunch tomorrow?**

4 Enter the body text

Subject: Lunch tomorrow?

Hi Eilidh, just wondered if you are around for lunch tomorrow?

Sent from my iPad

5 Tap once on the Send button to send the email to the recipient

Send

...cont'd

Mailboxes

Different categories of email messages can be managed via mailboxes. For instance, you may want to keep your social emails separately from ones that apply to financial activities. To use different mailboxes:

1 Tap once on this icon

2 The current mailboxes are displayed. Tap once on the Edit button

Hot tip

Messages can be edited within individual mailboxes. To do this, select a mailbox and tap once on the Edit button. The message can then be edited with the Delete, Move or Mark options at the bottom of the window.

3 Tap once on the New Mailbox button at the bottom of the Mailboxes panel

4 Enter a name for the new mailbox. Tap once on the Save button

5 Tap once on the Done button

6 To delete a mailbox, tap on it, then tap once on the Delete Mailbox button

Adding VIPs

One of the default Mailboxes is for VIPs, which can be used to store emails from your favorite contacts. To set this up:

1 When you get an email from someone you want to specify as a VIP, tap and hold on their name in the email header

2 Tap once on the Add to VIP button

3 Messages from VIPs are identified by a star next to them

> John Gillespie   10:29
> Re: iMac book
> Hi Nick! Just received your email - Internet problems. Very good to see you all and som...

4 Tap once on the VIP mailbox link to see the messages from all of your VIPs

★ **VIP**   ❯

Email threads

When you receive a number of emails on the same subject, as part of a conversation with one or more people, they can be sorted into threads, for easier viewing. To do this:

1 If there is an email thread, there is a number next to each email

> JOHN 📎   01/02/2012
> Pete's forthcoming anniversary
> Hi all Sounds good in theory.... More than happy to contribute. Thanks Joh...   **4** ❯

2 Tap once on the email to view the items in the full thread

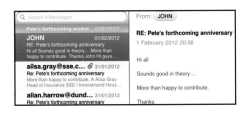

Having a Video Chat

Video chatting is a very personal and interactive way to keep in touch with family and friends around the world. The FaceTime app provides this facility with other iOS 5 and iOS 6 users on the iPad, iPhone and iPod Touch, or a Mac computer with FaceTime. To use FaceTime for video chatting:

1 Tap once on the FaceTime app

2 Sign in using your Apple ID to create your FaceTime account

To make video calls with FaceTime you need an active Internet connection.

3 Tap once on the Contacts button

4 Tap once on a contact to access their details for making a FaceTime call

5 Tap once on their phone number or email address to make a FaceTime call. The recipient has to have FaceTime on their iPad, iPhone, iPod Touch or Mac computer

6 Tap once on the Add to Favorites button to add the contact to your favorites list, for quick access

7 Once you have selected a contact, FaceTime starts connecting to them and displays this button

8 When you have connected, your contact appears in the main window and you appear in a picture-in-picture thumbnail in the corner

Hot tip

The contacts for FaceTime calls are taken from the iPad Contacts app. You can also add new contacts directly to the contacts list by tapping once on the + sign and adding the relevant details for the new contact.

89

9 Tap once on this button to swap between cameras on your iPad

10 Tap once on this button to end the FaceTime call

11 If someone else makes a call to you, tap once on the Decline or Accept buttons

Texting

Text messaging should not be thought of as the domain of the younger generation. On your iPad you can join the world of text with the Apple iMessage service that is accessed via the Messages app. This enables text and photo messages to be sent, free of charge, between users of the iOS 5 and iOS 6 operating systems, on the iPad, iPhone and iPod Touch. iMessages can be sent to cell/mobile phone numbers and email addresses. To use iMessages:

Beware

If a number, or an email address, is not recognized it shows up in red in the To box.

1 Tap once on this icon

2 Enter details for your location and your email address. Tap once on the Next button

3 Tap once on this button to create a new message and start a new conversation

4 Enter a phone number, or email address, here (this has to belong to an iOS 5 or 6 user)

5 Tap once on this button to select someone from your contacts

6 Tap once on a contact to select them as the recipient of the new message

Creating iMessages

To create and edit messages and conversations:

1 Tap once here and type with the keyboard to create a message. Tap once on the Send button

2 As the conversation progresses each message is displayed here

3 Tap once on this button to edit the messages in the current conversation

4 Tap once next to a message and tap once on Delete or Forward at the bottom of the window. Or, tap once on the Clear All button and tap once on the Clear Conversation button to delete the conversation

5 To edit whole conversations, tap once on the Edit button in the Messages panel

6 Tap once here and tap once on the Delete button to delete the conversation

Don't forget

When a message has been sent you are notified underneath it if it has been delivered.

Phoning with Skype

Skype is a popular app that is used on computers and mobile devices to make free phone and video calls. To do this, both users have to have Skype installed on their computer or mobile device and have a microphone and speakers attached, either internally or externally.

As well as making free calls to other Skype users, it is also possible to phone standard telephone numbers and, although there is a charge for this, it is often cheaper than standard phone charges.

To use Skype:

Downloading Skype

1   Access the App Store, enter Skype in the App Store Search box and tap once on the Skype for iPad link

2   Tap once here on the Skype app to download it

Using Skype
To make calls with Skype:

1   Tap once on the Skype icon

2   To use Skype you are required to register. This requires an email address and password

3   Enter your registration details and tap once on the Sign In button

4 Tap once on this button to search for contacts or add a telephone number of someone you know

5 Contacts are added here

6 Tap once on a contact to make a call

7 Tap once on the Voice Call button to make a call

8 Tap once on Video Call button to make a video call

9 Tap once on this button to mute the microphone

10 Tap once on this button to change the speaker volume

11 Tap once on this button to access the number pad for entering phone numbers

12 Tap once on this button to end a Skype call

93

Communication Apps

Within the App Store there is a range of communication apps that can be used to contact friends and family via text, phone and video. There are also several apps for sharing information, updates and photos. Some of these are:

- **Facebook.** The social networking phenomenon that has over a billion users around the world. This app enables you to create and use a Facebook account from your iPad. You can then interact with friends and family around the world by posting messages, comments and photos

- **Twitter.** Another of the top social networking sites on the Web. It provides the facility to post text or news messages of up to 140 characters. You can choose other users to follow, so you see their messages (tweets) and other people can follow you too

- **Flickr.** An iPad version of the popular photo- and video-sharing site. You have to register and once you have done this you can share your photos and videos with a vast online community

- **Pictures with Words.** Another photo-sharing app that enables you to share your photos online and also add captions, text and graphics to your images

- **WordPress.** A Web publishing app that can be used to create online blogs and also your own websites

- **Gmail.** If you have a Gmail account this will enable you to access it directly from your iPad

- **Windows Live Hotmail.** This can be used to access email from a Hotmail (or MSN or Live) account

- **Yahoo! Messenger.** This app is similar to Skype in that it offers free video and voice calling to other Yahoo! Messenger users

- **Talkatone for Google Voice and Facebook.** Another app for free phone calls and texts to phones in the USA and Canada

6 On a Web Safari

No computer experience is complete without access to the Web. This chapter shows how to use the iPad Web browser, Safari, to enjoy the online world.

Around Safari

The Safari app is the default Web browser on the iPad. This can be used to view Web pages, save favorites and read pages with the Reader function. To start using Safari:

1 Tap once on this icon

2 Tap once on the Address Bar at the top of the Safari window. Type a Web page address

Hot tip

When you type in the Safari Address Bar a .com key appears on the keyboard to make it quicker to enter website addresses.

3 Tap once on the Go button on the keyboard to open the Web page

4 Also, suggested options appear as you type. Tap once on one of these to go to that page

5 The selected Web page opens in Safari

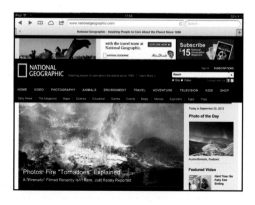

6 Swipe up and down and left and right to navigate around the page

Don't forget

Double-tap with one finger to zoom in on a page by a set amount. Double-tap with one finger to return to normal view. If the page has been zoomed by a greater amount by pinching, double-tap with two fingers to return to normal view.

7 Swipe outwards with thumb and forefinger to zoom in on a Web page (pinch inwards to zoom back out)

Safari Settings

Settings for Safari can be specified in the Settings app. To do this:

1 Tap once on the Settings app

2 Tap once on the Safari link

3 Tap once on the Search Engine link to select a default search engine to use

98

4 Tap once on the default search engine you want to use with Safari

5 Tap once here for options for filling in online forms

6 Drag this button to On to open new pages in the background of your current page

7 Drag this button to On to keep the Bookmarks Bar in view under the Address Bar in Safari

8 Drag the Private Browsing button to Off to disable this. If Private Browsing is On then no information will be recorded about visited websites

9 Tap once on the Accept Cookies link to specify how Safari deals with cookies from websites

10 Tap once on Clear History and Clear Cookies and Data to remove these items

11 Drag this button to On to enable alerts for when you have visited a fraudulent website

12 Drag these buttons to On to enable JavaScript files on websites and also block pop-up messages

Navigating Pages

When you are viewing pages within Safari there are a number of functions that can be used:

1 Tap once on these buttons to move forward and back between Web pages that have been visited

2 Tap once here to view bookmarked pages and also Reading List pages

3 Tap once here to add a bookmark, add to a reading list, add an icon to your iPad home screen, email a link to a page, tweet a page, send it to Facebook or print a page

4 Enter a keyword here to search for a topic

5 Tap once on a link on a page to open it. Tap and hold to access additional options, to open in a new tab, add to a Reading List or copy the link

6 Tap and hold on an image and tap once on Save Image or Copy

Opening New Tabs

Safari supports tabbed browsing, which means that you can open separate pages within the same window and access them by tapping on their tab at the top of the page:

1   Tap once here to open a new tab for another page

2   The page is opened in the new tab an untitled page. Access a website as shown on page 96

Access a website as shown on page 96

Don't forget

A maximum of nine tabbed pages can be used at the same time within Safari.

3   Tap once on the tab headings to move between tabbed pages

4   Tap once on the cross at the top of a tab to close it

Bookmarking Pages

Once you start using Safari you will soon build up a collection of favorite pages that you visit regularly. To access these quickly they can be bookmarked so that you can then go to them in one tap. To set up and use bookmarks:

1 Open a Web page that you want to bookmark. Tap once here to access the sharing options

2 Tap once on the Bookmark button

3 Tap once on this link and select whether to include the bookmark on the Bookmarks Bar or in a Bookmarks folder

4 Tap once on the Save button

5 Tap once here to view all of the bookmarks. The Bookmarks folders are listed. Tap once on the Edit button to delete or rename the folders

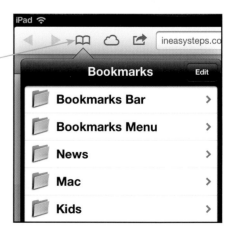

Safari Reader

The Safari Reader is a function that can be used to read individual items on a Web page without having any other of the content as a distraction:

1 In the Address Bar, if the Reader button appears it means that this function is available

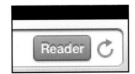

2 Tap once on the Reader button to view the page in this format

3 Rotate the screen to portrait to enable the text to fill more of the screen (images can be included on the Reader page, but only ones that relate to the article)

4 Tap once on the Reader button again to return to the standard page format

103

Don't forget

Not all Web pages have the Reader function. If the Reader button in Step 1 is not visible in the Address Bar then there is not a Reader function.

Hot tip

The text on the Reader page can be increased in size by tapping once on this icon at the top left-hand corner of the Reader page.

Web Apps

Although Safari can comfortably meet all of your Web browsing needs, there are a number of other browser apps that can be downloaded from the App Store. Many of these have a free (lite) version and there is sometimes a small charge for the full version. Generally, they have similar functionality but each has its own features too. It is worth looking at a few to compare the different interfaces. Some to try are:

- **Atomic Web Browser.** This is a browser that has a full-screen view, one-touch tabbed browsing and also a wider range of Multi-Touch Gestures for navigating

- **Dolphin Browser.** This browser has four different search engines from which to choose and Gestures and Sidebars for accessing pages quickly

- **Mercury Web Browser.** A stylish browser which includes customizable themes, ten-tab browsing, full-screen view and effective download options for links or images

- **Opera Mini Web Browser.** This is a fast browser that compresses data before downloading it for viewing. One of the fastest browsers available for the iPad

Beware

Flash is a video and animation format that is used widely on the Web. However, Flash video files cannot usually be played on the iPad.

- **SkyFire Web Browser.** This is an iPad browser with the unique feature of being able to play Flash video files. It does this by processing the content on its own servers and then sending it back to the browser. It is invaluable if you want to watch a lot of Flash video.

7 Staying Organized

An iPad is ideal for all of your organizational needs. This chapter shows how to use address books and calendars, keep notes and set reminders. It also details productivity apps for all of your everyday organizational needs.

Making Notes

It is always useful to have a quick way of making notes of everyday things, such as shopping lists, recipes or packing lists for traveling. On your iPad the Notes app is perfect for this function. To use it:

1 Tap once on this icon

2 Tap once on the note to access the keyboard. Start writing the note

3 Tap once on this button on the keyboard to hide the keyboard and finish the note. To edit an existing note, tap once on the text and the keyboard will reappear

4 As the note is created it appears in the Notes panel. The most recent note is at the top and the first line of the note is the title. Tap once on a note to view it

5 Tap once on this button to create a new note

6 Tap once on these buttons to, from left to right, move to the previous note, email or print a note, delete a note and move to the next note

Sending notes to iCloud

If you are using iCloud this can be used to send your notes to your iCloud email address. To do this:

1 Access the Settings app and tap once on the iCloud link

 iCloud

2 Drag the Notes button to On

Notes ON

3 In the Notes app, tap once on the Accounts button to view your iPad and iCloud notes

Accounts   3 Notes

4 Tap on the links to view the notes in those categories

Accounts

All Notes   >

On My iPad   >

iCloud   >

Beware

If iCloud is set up for Notes then all of your notes will appear in the iCloud account. If not they will all appear in the On My iPad account. Once in a specific account each note stays there, where it was created.

Setting Reminders

Another useful organization app is Reminders. This enables you to create lists for different topics and then set reminders for specific items. A date and time can be set for each reminder and, when this is reached, the reminder appears on your iPad screen. To use Reminders:

1 Tap once on this icon

2 The Reminder lists are located in the left-hand panel. Tap once on a list name

3 Tap once on a new line and enter the reminder

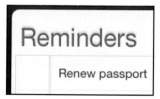

4 Hide the keyboard and tap once on the reminder to access the Details window

5 Drag this button to On

6 Tap once on the date and select a time and date for when you want the reminder alert

7 Tap once on the Done button

8 At the date and time of the reminder, a popup box appears

9 Tap once on the View button to see the details of the reminder

Using the Calendar

The built-in iPad Calendar can be used to create and view appointments and events. To do this:

1 Tap once on this icon

2 By default the calendar is displayed in a single day view, opening at the current day. Swipe left and right to view different days

Don't forget

If you have iCloud set up, the Calendar can be accessed through the website at www.icloud.com

3 Tap once here to view the calendar by Week, Month, Year or List view. Swipe left or right to move between days, weeks, months or years

4 Tap once on the Today button to view the current date. Tap once on the bar to move between dates

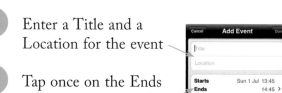

Hot tip

A new event can also be created in Day view. Tap and hold on a time slot to access the Add Event window.

5 Tap once on this button to create a new event

6 Enter a Title and a Location for the event

7 Tap once on the Ends link to set a timescale for the event

8 Drag on the barrels here to set an end time for the event. Tap once on the Done button

9 To invite other people to the event, tap once on the Invitees link (these will be people who you can select from your Contacts)

10 Tap once on this button

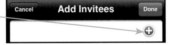

11 Tap once on a contact to select them

12 Tap once on the Done button. An email invitation will then be sent to the recipient's email address

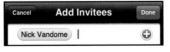

Your iPad Address Book

There is a built-in address book app on your iPad: Contacts. This enables you to store contact details which can then be used to contact people via email, iMessages or FaceTime. To add contacts:

1 Tap once on this icon

2 Tap once on this button to add a new contact

3 Enter the required details for a contact

4 Tap once on the Done button

5 Tap once on a contact to select them

6 Use these buttons to contact via text message (iMessage), video chat (FaceTime), share their contact details or add to your favorite contacts

7 Tap once on the Edit button to edit details in an individual entry

Edit

8 To delete a contact swipe to the bottom of the window in Edit mode and tap once on the Delete Contact button

Delete Contact

Hot tip

Tap once on a contact's email address to go directly to Mail to send them an email. Tap once on a cell/mobile phone number to access FaceTime for a video call (if the recipient is set up for this).

Don't forget

Contact details of an individual can be shared via email or as an iMessage.

Keeping Notified

Although the Notification Center feature is not an app in its own right, it can be used to display information from a variety of apps. These appear as a list for all of the items you want to be reminded about or be made aware of. Notifications are set up within the Settings app. To do this:

1 Tap once on this icon

2 Tap once on the Notifications link

3 The apps included in the Notification Center are listed here. Tap once on an app to edit its Notification Center settings

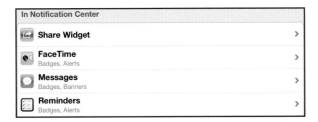

4 Drag this button On or Off to specify whether the selected item appears in the Notification Center

5 Drag downwards from the top of the screen to view the Notification Center

Don't forget

Tap once on an item in the Notification Center to view that item in its specific app.

Do Not Disturb

Although Notifications can be set so that you never miss a new message or alert, there may be times when you do not want to receive any calls or audio alerts. This can be done with the Do Not Disturb function.

Don't forget

The Do Not Disturb feature stops video FaceTime calls and also any audio alerts that have been specified in the Sounds section of the General app.

Hot tip

Activate the Repeated Calls option so that people can still contact you in an emergency, by placing successive FaceTime calls, separated by less than three minutes.

1 Open the Settings app and drag this button On

2 Tap once on Notifications

3 Tap once on this link

4 Drag the Scheduled button On, to specify a time period for when you do not want to be disturbed

5 Tap once on the Allow Calls from link to specify exception to Do Not Disturb

6 Select options for allowing calls (Favorites can be set for contacts in the Contacts app)

7 When Do Not Disturb is activated, a half-moon appears at the top of the screen at the point where the Notification Center is accessed

☾ 13:54

Organization Apps

In the App Store there is a wide range of organization apps for tasks such as note-taking. Some of these are:

- **Evernote.** One of the most popular note-taking apps. You can create individual notes and also save them into notebook folders. Evernote works across multiple devices so, if it is installed on other computers or mobile devices, you can access your notes wherever you are

- **Popplet.** This is an innovative note-taking app that enables you to link notes together, so you can form a mindmap-type creation. You can also include photos and draw pictures

- **Dropbox.** This is an online service for storing and accessing files. You can upload files from your iPad and then access them from other devices with an Internet connection

- **Bamboo Paper.** This is another note-taking app, but it allows you to do this by handwriting rather than typing. The free version comes with one notebook into which you can put your notes and the paid-for version provides another 20

- **Errands To-Do List.** A virtual To-Do list that can help keep you organized and up-to-date. You can create your own folders for different items and have alerts remind you of important dates, events and items

- **Notability.** Another app that utilizes handwriting for creating notes. It also accommodates word processing, and audio recording

- **Alarmed.** An app for keeping you on time and up-to-date. It has an alarm clock, pop-up reminders and pop-up timers

- **Grocery List.** Shopping need never be the same again with this virtual shopping list app

- **World Calendar.** Find out public holiday information for 40 countries around the world

Don't forget

Most organization apps are found in the Productivity category of the App Store.

Beware

For handwriting to work most effectively in Bamboo Paper, Multi-Touch Gestures should be turned Off in the Settings app.

Productivity Apps

If you want to do more than just use organization apps, there are some excellent productivity apps for creating word processing documents, presentations and spreadsheets. These can be used to write letters, produce holiday presentations or do household accounts. Some of the productivity apps are:

- **Pages.** This is a powerful word processing app that has been developed by Apple. It can be used to create and save documents which can then be printed or shared via email or copied to iTunes. There are a number of templates on which documents can be based. There is also a range of formatting and content options so it is possible to create engaging and eye-catching documents

- **Keynote.** Another Apple productivity app, this is a presentation app that can be used to create slides that can then be run as a presentation

- **Numbers.** This is the spreadsheet app that is part of the same suite as Pages and Keynote. Again, templates are provided or you can create your spreadsheets from scratch to keep track of expenditure or household bills. You can enter formulas into cells to perform simple, or complicated, calculations

- **Smart Office 2.** This app can be used to create, edit and share Microsoft Office documents, such as Word, Powerpoint and Excel. It supports all Microsoft Office versions since 1997 and also allows viewing of a variety of image files and PDF files

- **iA Writer.** A simple but effective word processing app. It creates documents that can be synchronized across other devices and also copied to iCloud or Dropbox

- **Free Spreadsheet.** This is similar to Numbers and although it does not have the same range of functionality it is still an effective spreadsheet

- **GoodReader for iPad.** This is an app for viewing PDF documents and large documents such as manuals or long books. It also has a facility for annotating PDF documents with text boxes, notes and drawings

Don't forget

PDF stands for Portable Document Format which is a file format created by Adobe to enable documents to be shared across different platforms without losing their formatting.

Saving Documents

For anyone who has grown up with computers and is used to a clear file structure, the first question when faced with an iPad is sometimes, 'Where do I save things?'. Unlike a Windows PC with Windows Explorer, or a Mac with the Finder, there is no obvious place to save files or create folders for content. This is because there isn't one. So where do you save your letters, presentations or photos once they have been created?

Self-contained saving

Instead of having a separate structure into which you can save files, content is saved within the apps in which they are created. So if you write a letter with the Pages word processing app, this is where is will be saved, and similarly if you create a note within the Notes app. Documents can be viewed as follows: (this is for Pages)

Hot tip

iPad apps save content automatically as it is being created so you do not have to remember to keep saving it as you work.

1 Tap once on the Documents button   **Documents**

2 All saved documents can be viewed here

3 When new documents are created they are added to this section. This is essentially the top-level folder

Adding folders

Despite the lack of a folder structure within the iPad operating system, folders can be created within some productivity apps, such as Pages. To do this:

1 Tap and hold on a document until it starts to jiggle. Drag it over another document icon

2 The new folder is created. Tap once here to give it a relevant name, then tap anywhere outside the folder to finish, or tap once on Done on the keyboard

Beware

You cannot create sub-folders, i.e. folders within folders. So the folder structure can only go down one level and you cannot copy one folder into another one.

119

3 The new folder appears in the main document area next to existing files

Printing Items

Printing from an iPad has advantages and disadvantages. The advantage is that it is done wirelessly so you do not have to worry about connecting wires and cables to a printer. The disadvantage is that there are a limited number of printers that work with the iPad printing system.

AirPrint

Content from an iPad is printed using the AirPrint system that is part of the iOS 5 and 6 operating systems. This is a wireless printing system that connects to your printer through your Wi-Fi network. However, there are a limited number of printers that are AirPrint-enabled so it may not work with your current printer.

AirPrint can print content from Safari, Mail, Photos, Pages, Keynote, Numbers and PDF documents in iBooks. Some third-party apps have AirPrint facilities but this depends on individual developers. To print items using AirPrint:

Don't forget

Check on the Apple website for a list of AirPrint-enabled printers.

1 Tap once on the tools option and select one of the Print options

2 Tap once on the Print link

Beware

Some developers offer third-party printing apps for the iPad. However, these work with varying degrees of success.

3 Select a printer or, if it has already been set up, tap once on the Print button to print

4 If your printer is not AirPrint compatible this will be shown in the Printer dialog box

8 Just Like a Good Book

This chapter looks at reading material on your iPad.

Newspapers and Magazines

With its portability and high-resolution Retina screen, the iPad is ideal for reading material from magazines and newspapers to books. The former can be downloaded and read with the Newsstand app and the latter with the iBooks app. To access reading material with the Newsstand:

Don't forget

There is a wide range of newspapers available through the Newsstand, usually specific to your geographical location.

1 Tap once on this icon

2 The Newsstand bookcase is initially empty. Tap once on the Store button to access the Newsstand store

3 The Newsstand Store is incorporated within the App Store. Items can be found in the main featured panel or by swiping left and right between items underneath the top panel

Beware

The majority of magazines and newspapers are initially free to download. However, most then require a paid-for subscription once the initial trial period for the item has expired.

4 When you have found a suitable magazine, newspaper or journal, review and download it in the same way as with an app in the App Store

5 Downloaded items appear on the Newsstand bookcase (Library). Tap once on a cover to open that publication

Hot tip

If there is a red circle with a number in it on the Newsstand app, this indicates available updates for your existing publications.

...cont'd

Reading magazines and newspapers

Once you have downloaded a publication you can then start browsing through it. To do this:

1 Tap once on an item on the cover to view it

Don't forget

Navigation toolbars differ slightly from publication to publication but they perform similar tasks.

2 Tap once on a page to access the top toolbar

3 Drag on this bar to move through the publication

4 Tap once on this button to view the publication's homepage

5 Tap once on this button to view the content of the current edition including cover page, table of contents and features

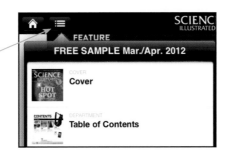

6 Tap once on this button to zoom in on a page. Tap once again to return to standard view

Hot tip

Pages can also be zoomed in on by using the Multi-Touch Gesture of swiping outwards with thumb and forefinger.
To zoom back in, pinch inwards with thumb and forefinger.

125

7 Tap once on this button to share the page by the available options, which can be by email, or sending to Facebook or Twitter

Finding Books

For anyone interested in reading, the iPad removes the need to carry around a lot of bulky books. If you are in the home, or traveling, you can keep hundreds of books on your iPad. This is done with the iBooks app, which can be used to download and read books across most genres: it is your own portable library. To use iBooks:

 Access the iBooks app in the App Store and download it in the same way as any other app

 Tap once on this icon once the iBooks app has been downloaded

Hot tip

Tap once on the Collections button to create new shelves under specific headings. These can be used to store books according to genre. Swipe left and right to move between collections.

3 The iBooks app interface consists of a bookcase, which initially is empty. Tap once on the Store button to access the iBooks store

4 Navigate through the iBooks Store in the same way as the App Store to find the required titles

5 Use these buttons to search for items within the iBooks Store (see pages 127-128)

Looking for books

The buttons at the bottom of the iBooks window can be used to look for books in different ways:

1 Tap once on this button to view the top selling books, for both paid-for and free books

Hot tip

A lot of classic books can be downloaded for free, as their copyrights have expired.

127

2 Tap once on this button to view different categories of books. Tap once on a category to view all of the books within it

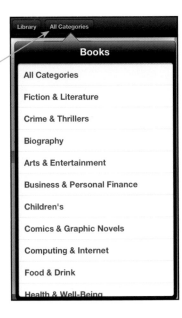

③ Tap once on this button to look for books by author. Tap once on an author's name to see their available titles and editions

Next to the Top Authors title, tap once on the Paid or Free buttons, to view authors and books for these criteria.

④ Tap once on this button to view the books that you have already downloaded or bought

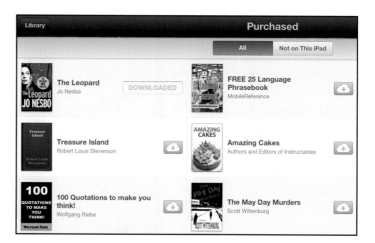

Downloading books

Once you have identified appropriate books they can then be downloaded to the iBooks bookcase (library). To do this:

1 Tap once on the book name or title to view its details

2 View the details of the book and any reviews (under the Ratings and Reviews heading)

129

3 Tap once on this button to download a sample of the book

4 Tap once here to download the book

£4.99

5 Downloaded books appear on the iBooks bookcase. Tap once on a book cover to open it and start reading

Reading Books

Reading an iBook

Once you have opened an iBook there are a number of ways to navigate and work with the content:

1 Tap once in the middle of a page in an iBook to access the top toolbar

2 Tap once on this button to return to the iBook Library (bookcase)

3 Tap once on this button to view the Table of Contents

4 Tap once on this button to change the text size

5 Tap once on this button to search for an item in the book

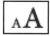

6 Tap once on this button to bookmark a page

7 Drag on this bottom bar to move through the book

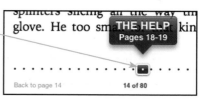

Working with text

When you are reading an iBook there are a number of options for enhancing the reading experience, from looking up dictionary definitions of words, to making notes about the text. To do this:

1 Tap and hold on a word to highlight it and access the text toolbar

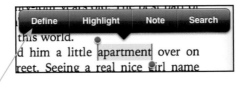

2 Tap once on the Define button to access a dictionary definition for the selected word. At the bottom of the window there are also options for searching the word over the Web or Wikipedia

Beware

If you use the Search Web or Search Wikipedia option, this takes you away from the iBook page.

131

3 Highlight a word and drag on the blue dots to extend the highlighted area

4 Tap once on the Highlight button and select an option for how the text is highlighted

5 Highlight a word and tap once on the Search button

6 The Search results show where the highlighted word appears in the book. Tap one of the instances to go to that section in the book

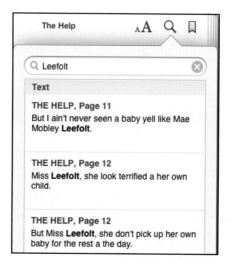

7 Highlight a word or phrase and tap once on the Note button

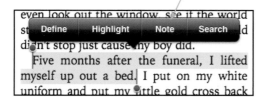

8 Enter your own note for the selected item

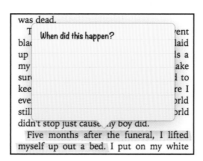

9 On the Table of Contents page, tap once on the Bookmarks button to view all of the bookmarked pages. Tap once on an item to view it

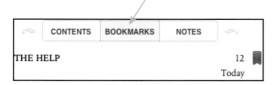

10 On the Table of Contents page, tap once on the Notes button to view all of the notes you have made in the book

Kindle on your iPad

The Kindle is the most popular eReader device for reading eBooks. However, it is now possible to use the Kindle app on your iPad. If you already have a Kindle account, on Amazon, then you can also import books that you have downloaded to your iPad. To use Kindle on your iPad:

134

1 Download the Kindle app from the Books category in the App Store

Kindle
AMZN Mobile LLC
Books
★★★☆☆ (7)

2 Tap once on this icon to open the Kindle app

Kindle

3 If you have a Kindle account, enter the details here to register your iPad Kindle. Tap once on the Register this Kindle button

kindle
nickvandome@mac.com
••••••••
Register this Kindle

4 Tap once on this button to view the titles that are in the Kindle Cloud, i.e. have been downloaded to your Kindle account on Amazon

Cloud

5 Tap once on this button to download a title from the Cloud to your iPad

6 Tap once on the Device button to view items that have been downloaded to your iPad

Beware

If you download a book from the Kindle Cloud it only appears under the Device button and not in your iBooks app.

135

7 Tap once on this button to view your books in list or icon view

8 Tap once on this button to sort your books by Most Recent, Title or Author

9 Tap once on this button to access Settings and other options for your Kindle on your iPad

...cont'd

Reading on the Kindle app

When you are reading a book on the Kindle app the options for navigating are similar to those for reading an iBook:

1 Tap once on this button to return to the main Library homepage

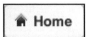

2 Tap once in the top right-hand corner of a page to add a bookmark

3 Tap once on these buttons to, from left to right, move to the previous page, search for an item in a book and view options for moving to various parts of the book such as table of contents and bookmarks

Don't forget

Tap once in the middle of a page to show or hide the toolbars.

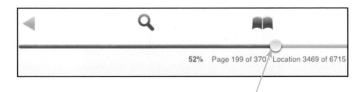

52%   Page 199 of 370   Location 3469 of 6715

4 Drag on this button to move through the book

5 Tap once on this button on the bottom toolbar to view options for the way the page is displayed. This includes text size and options for viewing black on white, white on black or sepia tone paper effect

6 If you are also reading books on a Kindle, tap once on this button on the bottom toolbar to synchronize your iPad version of the book with the Kindle one

9 Enjoying Leisure Time

The possibilities for enjoying yourself with your iPad are huge. This chapter looks at downloading and listening to music and capturing and using photos and videos in different creative ways. It also covers some lifestyle opportunities and shows how you can obtain apps for viewing art, drawing, health and cookery.

Buying Music

Music on the iPad can be downloaded and played using the iTunes and the Music apps respectively. iTunes links to the iTunes Store, from where music, and other content, can be bought and downloaded to your iPad. To do this:

1 Tap once on this icon

2 Tap once on the Music button on the iTunes toolbar at the bottom of the window

3 Use these buttons at the top of the window to find music

4 Tap once on an item to view it. Tap once here to buy an album or tap on the button next to a song to buy that individual item

5 Purchased items are included in the Music app's Library

Playing Music

Once music has been bought on iTunes it can be played on your iPad using the Music app. To do this:

1   Tap once on this icon

2   Use these buttons to find songs by different criteria

Hot tip

To create a Playlist of songs, tap once on the Playlist button, then tap once on the New button. Give it a name and then add songs from your Library.

3   Tap once on a track to select it and start it playing

4   Tap once on the middle button to pause/play a selected song

5   Drag this button to increase or decrease the volume

6   Tap once on this button to repeat a song or album after it has played

7   Tap once on this button to shuffle the order of songs

Hot tip

Music controls, including Play, Fast Forward, Rewind and Volume can be accessed by double-clicking the Home button on the iPad and swiping left to right on the Multitasking Bar.

Taking Photos

Because of its mobility and the quality of the Retina screen, the iPad is excellent for taking and displaying photos. Photos can be captured directly using one of the two built-in cameras (one on the front and one on the back) and then viewed, edited and shared using the Photos app. To do this:

Don't forget

The front camera on the iPad is an iSight 5 megapixel device. This is capable of capturing high-quality images and also HD videos.

Beware

Be careful to keep your fingers away from the camera lens when you are taking photos, particularly when you are using the camera on the other side of the iPad.

1. Tap once on the Camera app

2. Tap once on this button to capture a photo

3. Tap once on this button to swap between the front or back cameras on the iPad

4. Tap once on the Options button

5. Drag the Grid button to On to place a grid over the screen, if required. This can make it easier to frame photos by positioning items according to the lines in the grid

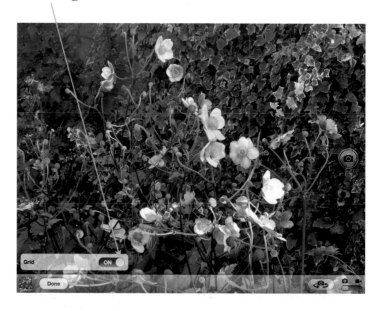

Viewing Photos

Once photos have been captured they can be viewed and organized in the Photos app. To do this:

1 Tap once on the Photos app

2 All photos, and videos that have been taken are shown here, under the Photos section

3 Tap once on a photo to view it at full-screen size

4 Swipe with one finger or drag here to move through all of the available photos

5 Tap once with two fingers to return the photo to its thumbnail size, or tap once on the Photos button

Hot tip

If you have iCloud set up, all of your photos will also be saved under the Photo Stream button. This enables all of your photos to be made available on any other devices you have with iCloud, such as an iPhone, an iPod Touch or a Mac computer.

Don't forget

To delete photos from the Photos section, tap once on the Edit button, tap once on an item to select it and tap once on the Delete button.

Edit

Working with Photos

Creating a slideshow

Photos can also be viewed in a slideshow format in the Photos app. To do this:

1 Tap once on the Slideshow button, either in the Photos section or when a photo is being viewed at full-screen size

2 Tap once on the Transitions link to select the way photos move between each other. Drag the Play Music button On or Off to select whether or not music is played. Tap once on the Start Slideshow button

Sharing photos

Within the Photos app there are a number of ways to share and use photos. To do this:

1 Open a photo at full size and tap once on this button

2 Tap once on one of the options for sharing the photo. These include emailing, adding to a contact in your Contacts app, using as your iPad wallpaper, tweeting, sending to Facebook, printing and copying the photo

Sharing with Photo Stream

The Photo Stream option can be used to share photos with other people with the Photo Stream Sharing function, or even give access to it through the Web through a public Photo Stream website:

Hot tip

To share multiple photos, access the main Photos section and tap once on the Edit button. Tap on photos to select them, tap once on the Share button and then follow from Step 3.

1. Select a photo you want to share via Photo Stream

2. Tap once on this button

3. Tap once on the Photo Stream button

4. Tap once on the New Photo Stream button

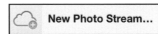

5. Enter a recipient with whom you want to share the Photo Stream and enter a name for it

Hot tip

If the recipient does not have an iCloud account, they can still view the Photo Stream by clicking on the View this Photo Stream on the Web link at the bottom of the email. This opens the photo(s) on an iCloud page that does not require login details, as long as the Public Website button in Step 5 is On.

6. Tap once on the Next button and enter a comment about the Photo Stream. Tap once on the Post button

7. The recipient receives an email inviting them to view the shared Photo Stream

143

...cont'd

Editing photos

The Photos app has options to perform some basic photo-editing operations. To do this:

1 Open a photo at full-screen size and tap once on the Edit button

2 Tap once on the Rotate button to rotate the photo 90 degrees at a time. Tap once on the Enhance button to have auto-color enhancements applied. Tap once on the Red-Eye button to remove red-eye in a photo. Tap once on the Crop button to crop an area of the photo

Creating albums

Within the Photo app it is possible to create different albums in which you can store photos. To do this:

1 Tap once on the Albums button

2 Tap once on this button

3 Enter a name for the new album

4 Tap once on the Save button

In the Photo Booth

The Photo Booth app is one of the built-in iPad apps that can be used to create fun, creative photo effects. To use it:

1   Tap once on this icon

2   The different special effects are shown through the camera. Tap once to select the desired effect

Hot tip

The Photo Booth app is a good one to use with grandchildren, who will enjoy experimenting with the special effects.

145

3   Check the image and capture it by tapping once on the camera button

Creating a Picture Frame

The iPad is such a thing of beauty that there is no reason why you should not make use of it even when you are not using it. The Picture Frame option enables you to display photos on the Retina screen when it is not in use:

1 Tap once on the Settings app

2 Tap once on the Picture Frame link

3 Select the settings for your Picture Frame

Don't forget

The Picture Frame has to be activated each time that the screen is locked, by tapping once on the button in Step 4.

4 When your iPad is locked, tap once on this button

5 Your photos are displayed according to the settings in Step 3

Capturing Videos

The iPad cameras can also be used to capture video, as well as photos. To do this:

1   Tap once on the Camera app

2   Drag this button to the right so that it is underneath the video camera icon

3   Tap once on this button to swap cameras from front to back

4   Tap once on this button to record a video. Tap once on it again to stop recording

Beware

Video can take up a lot of storage space on your iPad. For instance, a one minute video takes up approximately 80 MB of storage.

5   Once a video has been captured it is saved within the Photos app with the video camera icon and the duration of the video showing on the thumbnail. Tap once on this button to play a video

147

Viewing Videos

As the name suggests, the Videos app can be used to download and view video content. This is from the iTunes Store, rather than viewing your own videos. To do this:

1. Tap once on this icon

2. The Videos app is initially empty of content. Tap once here to access video content in the iTunes Store

3. Tap once on the Films button or the TV Programmes button

4. Tap once on an item to review its content. Tap once here to download it. This is usually in the form of buying or renting a video

5. The downloaded video appears in the Videos app. Tap once on the cover to view its contents

6. Tap once here to play a video

Photo and Video Apps

Within the App Store there is a category for Photo & Video, offering a range of apps for capturing and editing photos and videos. Some to try are:

- **iPhoto.** This is the iPad version of the popular Apple photo editing and organizing app. It is part of the iLife suite of apps and can be used as a photo library and also for a range of editing techniques, creating slideshows and sharing your photos

- **Adobe Photoshop Express.** A mobile version of the bestselling Photoshop suite of video editing apps. Multi-Touch Gestures can be used to apply a range of editing techniques including artistic filters

- **PowerCam HD.** A camera app that can be used to capture both photos and videos. Different special effects can be applied when the photos or videos are captured

- **360 Panorama.** This is an app that can be used to stitch your photos together to create a 360 degree view

- **Photo Collage HD.** An app for creating attractive collages with your photos. You can select and edit photos and add them to a collage with a range of backgrounds. It can then be shared via Facebook or Twitter

- **iMovie.** Another app from the Apple iLife suite. This is used to edit video that you have captured. It offers functions to trim video, add transitions, captions, music and voiceovers. Once the video has been edited it can then be shared via YouTube, Facebook or iTunes

- **Video Editor for FREE.** A video editing app that, as the name suggests, is free and a reasonable alternative to iMovie in terms of editing functionality

- **Video Downloader.** A useful app that can be used to play most video formats through a browser interface

- **Playable.** Another app for playing a wide range of video formats on your iPad

Discovering Art

It is always a pleasure to view works of art in real life, but the next best alternative is to be able to look at them on the high-resolution Retina display on your iPad. As far as viewing art goes, there are two options:

- Apps that contain general information about museums and art galleries

- Apps that display the works belonging to museums and art galleries

In general, type the name of a museum or art gallery into the App Store Search box to see if there is an applicable app. Some apps to look at are:

- **Guggenheim Bilbao.** Information and examples from the iconic museum in Bilbao

- **London Museums.** A general guide for finding museums in London. With an Internet connection it can be used to phone museums for booking

- **NYC Museum Guide.** Covering the museums of New York, this is a comprehensive guide including opening hours, bookings, maps and locations

- **Musée du Louvre HD.** High-resolution images and descriptions of the world-famous art of the Louvre

- **Museum Finder.** A general museum app for locating establishments around the world

- **50 painting masterpieces you must see in Madrid.** A detailed guide to the Prado Museum in Madrid, including descriptions of 50 famous paintings

- **Uffizi Touch.** Although this is more expensive than the other apps above, this offers a sumptuous tour of the works in the Uffizi Gallery in Florence

Creating Pictures

If you want to branch out from just looking at works of art, you can try creating some of your own too. There is a range of drawing and painting apps that can be used to let your creative side run riot. Most of these function in a similar fashion in terms of creating pictures:

1. Drawing tools appear at the bottom of the app

2. Swipe from left to right to access different tool options and selections

3. Tap and draw with your finger on the screen to create a picture

Some apps to try are:

- **Brushes.** One of the most powerful painting apps with a wide range of tools and features, including up to six layers in each painting and five blend modes

- **Drawing Pad.** Similar to Brushes, but at not such a high level. More suitable as a first option for iPad painting

- **Inspire Pro.** A wide range of blending features makes this one of the best painting apps around

- **Learn to Draw.** A drawing app that has tutorials for learning how to draw and also examples that can be used as templates and copied over

- **SketchBook Express.** A sketching app at a similar level to Brushes for painting

Hot tip

You may find using a touch screen stylus makes drawing easier

Don't forget

Most drawing and painting apps have an Undo function and also an eraser that can be used to remove unwanted items.

Cooking with your iPad

Your iPad may not be quite clever enough to cook dinner for you, but there are enough cookery apps to ensure that you will never go without a good meal with your iPad at your side. Some to look at are:

- **170,000+ Recipes.** As the name suggests, thousands of recipes to keep you busy in the kitchen for as long as you want. You can also store your grocery lists here

- **AllRecipes.** Enter a type of food, or dish, into the search box and see a variety of related recipes

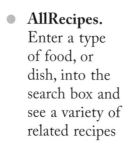

- **Cake Recipes.** To get your mouth watering, this app has hundreds of cake ideas, from the simple to the exotic

- **Green Kitchen.** A must for vegetarians, with stylish and creative recipes for organic and vegetarian food

- **iCake Italian.** If you cannot make it to Italy, bring a bit of Italy to your home with these recipes for cakes, pastries and tiramisu

- **Jamie's Recipes.** An app featuring the recipes of the well-known chef Jamie Oliver

- **Recipes Starter Kit.** For the less experienced chefs, this is a good way to gain confidence in the kitchen

- **Slow Cooker Recipes.** Put your dish together with this app, leave it in the slow cooker and then enjoy it several hours later when ready

- **Sweet Baking.** As well as covering cakes and cookies this app also has recipes for a variety of breads

Staying Healthy

Most people are health conscious these days and the App Store has a category covering Health & Fitness. This includes apps about general fitness, healthy eating, relaxation and yoga. Some to try are:

- **Calorie Counter and Diet Tracker.** If you want to stick to a diet this app can help you along the way. You need to register, which is free, and then you can set your own diet plan and fitness profile

- **Daily Workouts.** Some of the exercise apps are for dedicated gym-goers. If you are looking for something a bit less extreme this app could fit the bill. A range of exercises that will keep you fit without the need to be a body builder

- **Daily Yoga.** Audio and video instructions for timed sessions and over 30 yoga poses

- **Menu Planner.** A dieting aid that enables you to create your own menu plans

- **MyPilatesGuru.** Use this app to work through over 80 pilates exercise sessions. You can also create your own sessions and save them to repeat

- **Serenity.** Over 30 videos and sound files to help you relax or fall asleep

- **Sleep Pillow Ambiance.** Everyone enjoys a good night's sleep and this app can help you achieve it. A collection of ambient sounds are played to help you relax and sleep

- **Universal Breathing.** Designed to promote slow breathing, to help with a range of health conditions including high blood pressure, migraines and asthma

Don't forget

There is also a Medical category in the App Store that contains a range of apps covering medical topics.

Beware

If you have a genuine medical complaint, get it checked out by your doctor, rather than trying to find a solution through an app or on the Web.

Playing Games

Although computer games may seem like the preserve of the younger generation this is definitely not the case. Not all computer games are of the shoot-em-up or racing variety and the App Store also contains puzzles and versions of popular board games. There are two ways to access games:

- Via the App Store under the Games category

- Via the Game Center built-in iPad app. This is usually used if you want to compare scores with other users or if you want to play games simultaneously with other people online in a multi-player game

Some games to try are:

- **Chess.** Pit your wits against this chess app. Various settings can be applied for each game, such as the level of difficulty

- **Checkers.** Similar to the Chess app, but for Checkers (Draughts). Hints are also available to help develop your skills and knowledge

- **Mahjong.** A version of the popular Chinese game, but this is a matching game for single players, rather than playing with other people

- **Scrabble.** An iPad version of the best-selling word game that can be played with up to four people

- **Solitaire.** An old favorite, the card game where you have to build sequences and remove all of the cards

- **Sudoku.** The numbers game where you have to fill different grids with numbers 1-9, without having any of the same in a row or column

- **Tetris.** One of the original computer games, where you have to piece together falling shapes to make lines

- **Words With Friends.** Similar to Scrabble, an online word game, played with other users

Don't forget

As well as the games here, there is also a full range of other types of games in the App Store.

10 Getting on the Map

With an iPad, the Maps app and a Wi-Fi connection, the world is your oyster. This chapter shows how to find locations and directions.

Looking Around Maps

With the Maps app you need never again wonder about where a location is, or worry about getting directions to somewhere. As long as you are connected to Wi-Fi you will be able to do the following:

- Search maps around the world

- Find addresses

- Find famous buildings or landmarks

- Find the locations of the people in your Contacts app

- Get directions between different locations

- View traffic conditions

To ensure that the Maps app works most effectively, it has to be enabled for Location Services. To do this:

Beware

You can view maps without enabling Location Services, but this means that Maps will not be able to use your current location, or determine anything in relation to this.

1 Tap once on the Settings app

2 Tap once on this link

3 Tap once on the Location Services link

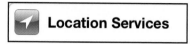

4 Drag the Location Services and Maps button to On

Viewing maps

Once you have enabled Location Services you can start looking around maps:

1 Tap once on this icon

2 Tap once on this button to view your current location

You can also zoom in and out on maps by swiping outwards with thumb and forefinger, or pinching inwards, respectively.

157

3 Double-tap with one finger on a map to zoom in

4 Tap once with two fingers on a map to zoom out

Finding Locations

Within Maps you can search for addresses, locations, landmarks, intersections or businesses. To do this:

1 Enter an item into the Search box

2 Tap once on the Search button on the keyboard

3 The required item is identified and shown on a map. Pins are also dropped at this point

Hot tip

You can also search for locations by postcodes or zip codes.

4 Locations can be viewed from a local, national or international level

Using Pins

Pins are used to identify locations and also display additional information about locations or addresses. They can also be used to access photos for a location.

In addition to pins that are dropped when you find a location, you can also drop your own pins at any point. To use pins:

1 Tap once on a pin to view its options

2 Tap once on this button to access additional information about the selected item

3 Tap once on these buttons to add an item to your Contacts, share it via email, iMessage, Facebook or a tweet or add to your Safari bookmarks

Don't forget

Tap on the Directions button on the pin options bar to find directions to the selected location.

4 To drop your own pin, tap and hold on a location. This drops a purple pin as opposed to the red ones. Tap and hold on a pin and drag it around to change its position

Getting Directions

Finding your way around is an important element of using maps and this can be done with the Directions function:

1 Tap once on the Directions button

2 By default, your current direction is used for the From field. If you want to change this, tap once and enter a new location or address

3 Enter a destination location or address

4 Tap once on this button to swap the locations

5 Tap once on the Route button on the keyboard (or at the top of the Directions window)

Route

6 The route is shown on the map

... cont'd

7 Tap once on the Start button to get directions

8 The route is shown on the map with directions for each section

161

Hot tip

Depending on the directions, the map will be zoomed in and out as you access each instruction.

9 Swipe to the left and right to view the next, or previous, set of directions for the route

Don't forget

To get back to the Start view, tap once on the End button.

...cont'd

10   Tap once on this button in the bottom left-hand corner of the screen to view details of the route for the selected mode of transport. The default option is by car

Beware

Directions for public transport are not usually given between two destinations in different countries.

11   Tap once on this button and tap once on the Route button to find options via public transport

12   Tap on an app to download it for a specific mode of transport. This can then be used in conjunction with a route in the Maps app

13   Tap once on this button to view the directions by foot

Finding Contacts

As well as looking for locations and landmarks, it is also possible to find locations and directions for people in your address book (Contacts app). To do this:

1 Tap once on this button

2 Tap once on a contact in your Contacts app

3 If there is no address entered for the contact this will be displayed in the Info window

4 If there is an address associated with the contact, this will be displayed on a map and a pin will be dropped

Don't forget

Tap once on the image button on the pin toolbar, to see a photo of the contact's home or location.

Types of Maps

The standard view that is used in Maps can be changed so that you can view maps according to satellite and hybrid views. To do this:

 Swipe inwards here to access the map options

 Tap on the buttons in the corner to select the map types (Standard, Hybrid and Satellite). Swipe the turned-up map into the corner to return to map view

Using Flyover

One of the innovative features in the Maps app is the Flyover function. This enables you to view locations, in 3D relief, as if you were moving over them from above. You can also zoom in and change the perspective. To use Flyover:

1 Access a map and select the Satellite option

2 Tap once on this button to activate the Flyover functionality (if available for the area being viewed)

3 The perspective changes so you are viewing the map from an angle

The Flyover function is only available for certain cities around the world, with the majority being in the USA. However, this number is increasing regularly. If Flyover is not available, the button in Step 2 is 3D.

...cont'd

 Zoom and swipe to 'fly over' the map (zoom in by pinching together with thumb and forefinger)

Swivel the map by turning in a circular fashion with thumb and forefinger, to view it from a different perspective

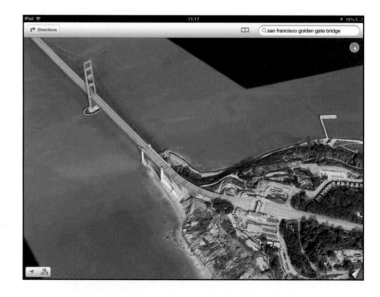

11 Traveling Companion

This chapter shows why you should never be without your iPad when you are traveling or on vacation.

Traveling with your iPad

When you go traveling, there are a few essentials that you have to consider: passport, money and insurance to name three. To this you can add your iPad: it is a perfect traveling companion that can help you plan your trip and keep you informed and entertained when you are away from home.

Uses for traveling

There are a lot of App Store apps that can be used for different aspects of traveling. However, the built-in apps can also be put to good use before and during your travels:

- **Maps.** Use this app for accessing maps of your destinations, finding directions and viewing images of areas to which you are traveling

- **Notes.** Create items such as lists of items to pack or landmarks that you want to visit

- **Contacts.** Keep your Contacts app up-to-date so that you can use it to send postcards to friends and family. You can also use it to access phone numbers if you want to phone home

- **Reminders.** Set reminders for important tasks, such as changing foreign currency, buying tickets and details of flights

- **Music.** Use this app to play your favorite music while you are traveling, or relaxing at your destination

- **Photos.** Store photos of your trip with this app and play them back as a slideshow when you get back home

- **FaceTime.** If you have a Wi-Fi connection at your destination you will be able to keep in touch with video calls (as long as the recipient has FaceTime too)

- **iBooks.** Instead of dragging lots of heavy books around, use this app for your vacation library

Hot tip

The Clock app can also be used so that you can keep an eye on the time in different parts of the world.

Beware

You can also use the Videos app to download movies and TV shows from the iTunes Store. However, these will take up a significant amount of space on your iPad in terms of storage.

Planning your Trip

A lot of the fun of going on vacation and traveling is in the planning. The anticipation of researching new places to visit and explore can whet the appetite for what is ahead. The good news is that you can plan your whole itinerary while sitting in an armchair with your iPad on your lap. In the App Store there are apps for organizing your itinerary and others for exploring the possibilities of where you can go:

Tripit

This is an app for keeping all of your travel details in one place. You have to register, which is free, and you can then enter your own itinerary details. Whenever you receive an email confirmation for a flight, hotel or car hire that you have booked, you can email this to your Tripit account (plans@tripit.com) and this will be added to your itinerary.

GetPacked

A great way to get peace of mind before you leave. This app generates a packing list and to-do lists to check before you leave, based on questions that you answer about your

Don't forget

Although there is a small fee for the GetPacked app, it is well worth it as it covers everything you will need to consider before you leave.

vacation and travel arrangements. You can then select items to include on your packing list, from clothes to documents and medical items.

...cont'd

Cool Escapes

Guaranteed to give you itchy feet, this app matches quality hotels with some amazing locations around the world.
You can explore by map, country, area, hotel type and price, to find the perfect combination.

Beware

Some maps apps are free to download but there is then a fee to buy the associated maps.

World Travel Atlas

A comprehensive travel companion which offers a world atlas that contains information about countries, cities, landmarks, airports and events. Navigate around the atlas with the same swiping and tapping gestures as with the Maps app. Tap once on an item to access a wealth of information about it.

Viewing Flights

Flying is a common part of modern life and although you do not have to book separate flights for a vacation (if it is part of a package) there are a number of apps for booking flights and also following the progress of those in the air:

Skyscanner
This app can be used to find flights at airports around the world. Enter your details such as leaving airport, destination and dates of travel. The results show a range of available options, covering different price ranges.

FlightRadar24
If you like viewing the path of flights that are in the air, or need to check if flights are going to be delayed, this app provides this inflight information. Flights are shown according to flight number and airline.

Flight apps need to have an Internet connection in order to show real-time flight information.

AirportZoom
As well as showing real-time flight details, this app also has airline departure and arrival information and maps of airport terminals and flight gates.

FlightAware
Another app for tracking flights, showing arrivals and departures and also information about delays.

Finding Hotels

The Internet is a perfect vehicle for finding good value hotel rooms around the world. When hotels have spare capacity, this can quickly be relayed to associated websites, where users can usually benefit from cheap prices and special offers. There are plenty of apps that have details of thousands of hotels around the world, such as:

TripAdvisor

One of the top travel apps, this not only has hotel information but also restaurant, activities and flights. Enter a destination in the search box and then navigate through the available options.

Hotels.com

A stylish app that enables you to enter search keywords or tap once on a hotel on the homescreen to view options for this location.

Hot tip

Most hotel apps have reviews of all of the listed establishments. It is always worth reading these as it gives you a view from the people who have actually been there.

Booking.com

Another good, fully-featured hotel app that provides a comprehensive service and excellent prices.

iRooms@LateRooms.com

An app that specializes in getting the best prices by dealing with rooms that are available at short notice. Some genuine bargains can be found here, for hotels of all categories.

Converting Currency

Money is always important in life and never more so than when you are on vacation and possibly following a budget. It is therefore imperative to know the exchange rate of currencies in different countries compared to your own. Two apps that provide this service are:

XE Currency

This app delivers information about exchange rates for all major world currencies and also a wealth of background information such as high and low rates and historical charts.

Hot tip

When changing currency, either at home or abroad, always shop around to get the best rate. Using credit cards abroad usually attracts a supplementary charge too.

173

Currency

This app provides up-to-date exchange rates for over 150 currencies and 100 countries.

Travel Apps

Everyone has different priorities and preferences when they are on vacation. The following are some apps from the App Store that cover a range of activities and services:

- **1000 Places To See Before You Die.** A collection of stunning and unforgettable destinations and locations around the world. Impressive photography makes it all the more appealing and you can also browse maps

- **Disneyland Paris.** If you are entertaining your grandchildren at Disneyland Paris, this app will help you survive the experience. Maps, show times and descriptions of features help you organize all aspects of your visit

- **Fotopedia Heritage.** A selection of stunning photography of World Heritage sites. Guaranteed to make you want to head for the airport

Don't forget

Fotopedia has other photography apps, covering areas including National Parks, Wild Friends and Women of the World.

- **Florida Theme Parks.** Another one for the family and grandchildren. Everything you need to know about these popular tourist attractions

- **Google Earth.** Not just a travel aid, this app enables you to search around the globe and look at photos and 3D maps of your favorite places

- **Hailo.** For anyone visiting London, Dublin or Toronto, this app allows you to hail a cab, at the tap of a button

- **Kayak.** A useful all-round app that compares hundreds of travel websites to get the best prices for flights, hotels and car rental. You can also create your own itineraries

- **Language apps.** If you want to learn a new language for your travels, there is a wide range of apps for this. These are located in either the Travel or Education categories in the App Store

- **Laplication.** For something a little bit off the beaten track, use this app to see the wonders of Lapland, including the incredible Northern Lights

- **myLanguage Free Translator.** If you do not have the time, or inclination, to learn a new language, try this app to translate 59 different languages

- **National Geographic Traveler.** Subscribe to this app to get an endless supply of high-quality travel features, photography and travel ideas

- **New York Subway Map.** Use this app to help get around the Big Apple via the Subway. Plan your journeys and view live updates about stations and routes

Don't forget

There are apps for displaying train times and details, but these are usually specific to your geographical location rather than covering a range of different countries.

175

...cont'd

- **Over 40 Magnifier and Flashlight.** Not just for traveling, this fantastic app acts as a torch and a magnifying glass all in one

- **P&O Cruises.** Find some of your favorite cruises with this app that displays the full brochure of P&O Cruises

- **Paris Transport Map.** One free map for travel options around one of the great cities in the world

- **Photo Translator.** Ever wondered what signs in a foreign language mean? This app can translate them for you: take a photo with your iPad and the app gives you a translation of the sign, or phrase

- **Phrasebook.** Keep up with what the locals are saying in different countries with this app that has useful phrases in 25 languages

- **Sixt Rent a Car.** Use this app for car rental in 90 countries around the world

- **London Tube Map.** Find your way around London with this digital version of the iconic Tube Map. It includes live departure boards and station information

- **Urbanspoon.** Another app for finding restaurants on your vacation. Enter your location, shake your iPad and the app uses a slot machine interface to come up with suggestions. Covers USA, Canada, UK and Australia

- **Weather+.** An app for showing the weather in locations around the world, including background videos and hourly updates

- **Wi-Fi Finder.** It is always useful to be able to access Wi-Fi when you are on vacation, and sometimes essential. This app locates Wi-Fi hotspots in 650,000 locations in 144 countries worldwide

- **Yelp.** Covering a range of services, this app locates restaurants, shops, services and places of interest in cities around the world

12 Practical Matters

This chapter looks at security issues on the iPad and also shows how to use it for financial issues and buying property.

Setting Restrictions

Within the iPad Settings app there are options for restricting types of content that can be viewed and also actions that can be performed. These include:

- Turning off certain apps so that they cannot be used
- Enabling changes to certain functions
- Restricting content that is viewed using specific apps

When setting restrictions, they can be locked so that no-one else can change them. To set and lock restrictions:

1 Tap once on the Settings app

2 Tap once on the General tab

3 Tap once on the Restrictions link

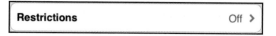

4 The restrictions are grayed-out, i.e. they have not been enabled for use yet

5 Tap once on the Enable Restrictions link

Enable Restrictions

6 Type on the keypad to set a passcode for enabling and disabling restrictions

7 Re-enter the passcode

8 All of the Restrictions options become available. Drag these buttons On or Off to disable certain apps. If this is done they will no longer be visible on the Home screen. Tap once on the links under Allowed Content to specify restrictions for certain types of content, such as music, movies and apps

Beware

If you forget the passcode for unlocking your iPad it will become disabled for a period of time after you have entered the wrong passcode a number of times. Eventually, it will lock completely. It can be reset by using a computer with which the iPad was last synced and there are details about this on the Apple website Support pages. However, to avoid this, ensure that you have a note of the iPad's passcode, but keep it away from the iPad.

Finding your iPad

No-one likes to think the worst, but if your iPad is lost or stolen, help is at hand. The Find My iPad function (operated through the iCloud service) allows you to send a message and an alert to a lost iPad and also remotely lock it or even wipe its contents. This gives added peace of mind, knowing that even if your iPad is lost or stolen its contents will not necessarily be compromised. To set up Find My iPad:

1 Tap once on the Settings app

2 Tap once on the iCloud link

3 Drag this button to On to be able to find your iPad on a map and send messages to it remotely

4 Tap once on the Allow button to enable the Find My iPad functionality

Finding a lost iPad

Once you have set up Find My iPad you can search for it through the iCloud service. To do this:

1 Login to your iCloud account at www.icloud.com

2 Tap once on the Find My iPhone button (this also works for the iPad)

Hot tip

Location Services has to be turned On to enable the Find My iPad functionality. This is done in the Settings app. Tap once on the Location Services link and tap once on the Find My iPad link.

180

3 Tap once on the Devices button and select your iPad. It is identified and its current location is displayed on the map

4 Tap once on the green circle to view details about when your iPad was located

Don't forget

Click once on the Erase iPad button to delete the iPad's contents.

5 Tap once here to send a sound alert to your iPad

6 Tap once here to lock your iPad

7 Enter a passcode so that no-one else can access the contents on your iPad

Locking your iPad

As shown in Chapter Two, the screen can be auto-locked, but this does not have a security control. If you want to make sure that no-one else can access your iPad's content a passcode can be set for unlocking the screen. To do this:

1. Tap once on the Settings app

2. Tap once on the General link General

3. Tap once on the Passcode Lock button

   Passcode Lock   Off >

4. Tap once on the Turn Passcode On link

   General   Passcode Lock
   Turn Passcode On
   Change Passcode
   Require Passcode   Immediately >
   Simple Passcode   ON

5. Enter the passcode and re-enter it to confirm it

6. The passcode has to be entered to access the iPad for use every time it has been locked

Avoiding Viruses

As far as security from viruses on the iPad is concerned there is good news and bad news:

- The good news is that, due to its architecture, most apps on the iPad do not communicate with each other so, even if there was a virus, it is unlikely that it would infect the whole iPad. Also, there are relatively few viruses being aimed at the iPad, particularly compared to those for Windows PCs

- The bad news is that no computer system is immune from viruses and malware, and complacency is one of the biggest enemies of computer security. Also, as iPads become more popular they will become a more attractive target for hackers and virus writers

iPad security

Apple takes security on the iPad very seriously and one way that this manifests itself is in the fact it is designed so that different apps do not talk to each other. This means that if there was a virus in an app then it would be hard for it to transfer to others and therefore spread across the iPad. Apple's own apps are the exception to this, but as they are developed and checked by Apple there is very little chance of them being infected by viruses.

Antivirus options

There are a few apps in the App Store that deal with antivirus issues, although not actually removing viruses, due to the lack of iPad viruses in circulation. Some options to look at:

- **VirusBarrier.** This checks files that are copied onto your iPad, via email or online services, to ensure that they are virus-free

- **McAfee Global Threat Intelligence Mobile.** This is not technically an antivirus app, but it does provide a daily update about new viruses that are in circulation

- **Anti-Virus Detective.** This is an app that has a step-by-step process for identifying suspected viruses or malware

Don't forget

Malware is short for malicious software, designed to harm your computer or access and distribute information from it.

Don't forget

Apple also checks apps that are provided through the App Store and this process is very robust. This does not mean that it is impossible for a virus to infect the iPad (but there have not been any so far) so keep an eye on the Apple website to see if there are any details about iPad viruses.

Dealing with Money

We all like to keep track of our money and, although it may not be as much fun as reading books or looking at photos, it is a necessary task that can be undertaken on the iPad.

Some general financial apps are looked at on page 186, but one of the most common uses for financial matters is online banking. This is where you can use banking apps to access your bank accounts.

Banking apps are specific to your geographical location, i.e. the banks that operate in your country. Most banking apps operate in a similar way:

Some general financial apps are looked at on page 186

Beware

If you are logging into your online banking service, make sure any Remember Me log in details functions are checked off, particularly if other people have access to your iPad.

Don't forget

Online banking sites can also be accessed through the Web using Safari.

1   You have to first register for the online service. Once you have done this tap on the Log On button to access your account details

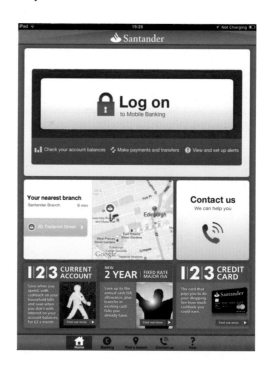

2   General information is also available through the app, such as branch locations and contact details

Looking at Property

If you are looking to move home, or buy property as an investment, your iPad is a great starting point. There are a lot of real estate apps that provide high quality color photos of all parts of properties for sale.

As with banking apps, real estate apps are specific to your geographical location and they all have a search facility for looking for properties in different areas. The search results can usually be filtered by criteria such as price, number of bedrooms and property type. To use a real estate app:

1 Browse properties according to area

Don't forget

Some property apps also allow you to book appointments to view properties in person.

185

2 Tap once on a property to view more details. This usually includes photos of all of the rooms and a full description of the property

Financial Apps

Within the Finance category of the App Store there are apps for managing your personal finances, viewing share prices and organizing your bank accounts and bills. Some to look at are:

- **Account Tracker.** A useful app for keeping track of your expenditure. It can be used to monitor multiple bank accounts and also set alerts and reminders for paying bills

- **Calculator.** For working out your own finances, this calculator provides a large, attractive interface with plenty of functionality

- **Bloomberg.** This is an app for following stocks and shares. You can add any shares that you own and view live prices while markets are open (with a 15 minute delay). There is also a news service with related financial details

- **HomeBudget.** An app for managing your household incomes and expenses. It also supports charts and graphs so you can compare expenditure over periods of time

- **Meter Readings.** Useful for keeping an eye on your fuel consumption, this app helps you to save money by monitoring your utility readings. Enter the readings and your usage and costs are displayed in user-friendly graphs to show where savings can be made

- **Mint.com.** Another general finance app for managing your money and monitoring budgets

- **Money for iPad Free.** As well as being used to manage bills and view all of your accounts, this app also provides useful planning features and reminders

- **Pocket Expense.** Another in the range of apps with which you can monitor bank accounts, track bills, view transactions and see where you can save money

- **SharePrice.** Another app for seeing how your share portfolio is doing. Real-time share information, market news and profit/loss details are provided

Hot tip

With your iPad and an Internet connection, you should always be able to keep an eye on your shares portfolio as well as buying and selling shares, wherever you are.

Index